Collected A

Awareness to Action Leadership

By Mario Sikora

Awareness to Action International
ISBN-10: 1521358036
ISBN-13: 978-1521358030
©2017 Mario Sikora
All Rights Reserved

About the Author

Mario Sikora is president of the leadership-consulting firm Awareness to Action International and an executive coach. For nearly 20 years he has advised leaders in large organizations across the globe.

An internationally recognized speaker and author, Mario is co-author of the book "Awareness to Action: The Enneagram, Emotional Intelligence, and Change" and author of many articles on personality styles and leadership, performance improvement, and teambuilding. His writings have been translated into Italian, Spanish, French, Turkish, Portuguese, Arabic, Russian, Korean, and Danish.

Mario specializes in working with senior leaders in a number of areas, including:

• *Performance turnaround*—helping leaders overcome performance patterns that are undermining their success.

• *Scaling for broader assignments*—helping high-potential leaders adjust to or prepare for the demands of a larger assignment.

• *Global leadership*—helping clients succeed in global roles that require multi-cultural skil*l*.

• *Leadership and Talent Development*—helping clients develop the two most important tasks of leadership—influencing and motivating others and developing strong leaders in their wake.

• *Team Building and Team Coaching.*

Mario is an internationally recognized expert and thought-leader in the Enneagram model of personality styles. He has taught the Enneagram in companies and to public audiences on five continents, and he delivers Enneagram certification programs for coaches, consultants, and human-resources and organizational-development professionals.

Before forming Awareness to Action International, Mario held various roles in publishing and corporate communications. He lives outside of Philadelphia with his wife and their four sons.

Awareness to Action International is an international consulting group that helps our clients develop the kind of practical self-awareness that leads to effective action.

Our consultants come from a wide variety of industry backgrounds, from international banking to telecommunications to publishing, giving us a unique breadth and depth of experience. Our experience with the Enneagram model of personalities styles in working with—and getting results in—organizations throughout the world is hard to match.

We work with organizations of all sizes—from small regional companies to non-profits to multibillion-dollar international corporations. We have experience working with leaders and teams on five continents and bring a multi-cultural mindset to our engagements.

We are proud of the results we deliver to our clients, and we take pride in the fact that we are always learning from them, developing our own awareness and insights so we can better help you.

ATAI specializes in working with senior leaders in a number of areas, including:

• *Scaling for broader assignments*—helping high-potential leaders adjust to or prepare for the demands of a larger assignment.

• *Global leadership*—helping clients succeed in global roles that require multi-cultural skill.

• *Leadership and Talent Development*—helping clients develop the two most important tasks of leadership—influencing and motivating others and developing strong leaders in their wake.

ATAI helps prepare leaders for the future by weaving together the most useful insights from cognitive and evolutionary psychology, leadership and management theory, and personality studies and combining them with nearly two decades of real-world experience working with leaders in organizations of all sizes across the globe.

Contact us at:

info@AwarenessToAction.com

www.AwarenessToAction.com

+1.215.825.2501

Table of Contents:

Curiosity

Creativity

Process/Structure

Developing Talent and Network

Appropriate Self-Promotion

Collected Articles, Vol. 1
Awareness to Action Leadership
By Mario Sikora

Introduction

"Awareness to Action Leadership" is as much an attitude as it is a model for leadership. At its core is the belief that effective leadership starts with *awareness*— self-awareness, an understanding of others, and the ability to see our environment with as few distortions and filters as possible. Building upon awareness is *authenticity*—the willingness and ability to adapt to our environment; the capacity to change, but to change in a way that stays true to our fundamental values and temperament. Finally, and one could argue most importantly, comes the ability to take *action*—to act effectively and efficiently, to execute, and to drive execution throughout the organization.

I have developed a leadership model over the past 15 years that identifies 12 competencies separated into four groups, with each group represented by a simple, dynamic model.* These are competencies that I have I have found to be useful to be useful to my clients—leaders of large and small organizations on five continents. The articles in this collection, to the degree possible, are divided into sections relating to those 12 competencies. They are articles that I have written over the past five years or so, and they were not written with the plan to eventually gather them in a collection such as this. Therefore, I will ask the reader's forgiveness for the overlap and redundancies in some of the articles, but each article included adds some value that is not found in other articles in the collection.

The nature of this collection also is such that the reader can dip in at any point and skip around at will. While I recommend reading the first article first, beyond that pick and choose as you wish; each article stands alone (except for the few that are indicated).

An e-reader version of this collection will follow soon; for information on its availability, please send an email to info@AwarenessToAction.com.

These articles include many of the ideas explored in our programs. Awareness to Action International is a truly international company, with a presence of four continents. We are leading experts on the interface of personality and performance, and that expertise is applied to our executive coaching, teambuilding, and leadership-development programs.

You can find out more about our programs by visiting our website at www.AwarenessToAction.com. For a copy of our brochure, send a request to info@AwarenessToAction.com.

*As I explain in the opening article, no leadership model is complete and no set of competencies is exhaustive when it comes to the skills and abilities needed by leaders. The Awareness to Action Leadership model is simply a useful skeleton upon which a leader can continue to build.

Awareness to Action Leadership

(This article serves as the introduction to the Awareness to Action International Executive Coaching Guidebook, which is available to ATAI clients.)

It's pretty clear what leaders must do.

> They must:
>
> 1. Express a vision
> 2. Build and leverage relationships
> 3. Think strategically
> 4. Drive execution
> 5. Empower others

What's less clear is who leaders are—the skills, attributes, or attitudes they possess that help them effectively do the things listed above.

Awareness to Action Leadership is an approach to helping leaders understand the "who" of leadership and develop those skills, attributes, and attitudes so they can excel at the act(s) of leading. We do this with the help of four simple leadership models that help our clients develop the self-awareness and broad competencies that can support whatever specific skills are needed for a particular leadership situation.

This guidebook covers those models and is designed to help leaders grow beyond their current limitations and learn to do at a higher level.

But first, some thoughts on leadership that will help the reader understand our attitudes about leadership.

There are as many definitions of leadership as there are leaders and people writing about leaders, but this one works for us: successful leadership is the act of influencing others to effectively achieve a desired result consistently and over time. There are a couple of assumptions implicit in this definition, namely that leadership involves the engagement of others, that good leadership improves circumstances, and that in order to get results over time one must lead in a way that makes others want to follow. Thus, treating people well is inherently more effective than treating them poorly.

Here are some opinions we've formed about leaders and leadership:

There is no secret formula.

Leadership is very context specific; what works in one situation for one person may not work in another situation, or even for a different person in the same situation. Effective leadership requires adaptability to the variables of individuals, contexts, and goals. Circumstances may require a leader to call upon any of a very long list of skills, competencies, attitudes, or behaviors. The challenge is that we can never know in advance what those variables may be at any given time. Thus, a leader must be a student of leadership, continually improving his or her abilities, and constantly monitoring the environment for cues as to what abilities need to be developed. There is a quote commonly attributed to Charles Darwin that is true of leadership: "It is not the strongest of the species that survives, nor the most intelligent, but the one most responsive to change."

Because there is no secret formula, we should always beware those who promise a secret formula. Beware of any consultant, coach, or trainer who tells you that his or her list of competencies is complete or "necessary and sufficient."

Leaders are "born" and "made."

Not born, perhaps, but there does seem to be some innate set of intangible qualities that many leaders have that non-leaders don't. We don't know whether they are born with these qualities or whether they are the result of early experience, but the qualities tend to already be in place by the time the leader gets to adulthood.

That said, almost anyone—given the requisite intelligence, drive, and fundamental task competence related to their job—can improve their leadership ability. Not everyone is a born leader, but everyone can become a better leader than they are now.

Good leaders have an almost-compulsive need to lead.

For whatever reason, the best leaders seem unable to *not* lead. Some lead out of a desire to achieve their personal goals, some lead for the rewards of the position, but the best can't explain why they want to lead; they just have some inner drive pushing them toward the front. They often report a desire to see results or shape their environment, and they often feel that they must do it because no one else is as capable or willing. Others sense this drive in them and unconsciously follow. Whatever the (often post-hoc) rationale, the need to lead seems to come from an irresistible urge deep in the psyche.

Good leaders work harder than most people.

Delegation, working at the right level, and some degree of work/life balance are important leadership qualities. However, the best leaders love the job of leading and put countless hours into doing it well. They think about work almost all the time; they are constant learners, always seeking to improve; they are willing to get on a plane and fly across the world, to start the day early and to end it late. Good leaders might fail because they are outsmarted or because they didn't have the right skills or the right team or the right product they needed for the circumstances, but they will never fail because they didn't work hard enough.

Leaders are (and should be) judged on results.

There seem to be two broad camps when it comes to leadership theory; one can be called the "hard-line" camp and the other the "soft-line" camp. The latter is focused on what are traditionally called "soft-skills," interpersonal skills, empowerment, teamwork, etc. The hard-line camp, more dominant among senior business leaders, focuses on getting bottom-line results. Soft skills matter, but primarily because they are usually needed to get results over the long term (and secondarily because being nice to people is simply good form). A leader can browbeat people into getting results for a while, but eventually people (the good ones, at least) leave or fail to perform at a high level. *Sustainable leadership uplifts and motivates people in positive ways.* But it is a mistake to neglect the cold, hard facts of life as a leader: if you do not get the results you have been hired to get, you have failed and you will not be the leader for very long. A good leader is able to keep results at the forefront of everyone's concerns and perform some of the unpleasant actions necessary to get the results (reducing costs and inefficiencies, firing underperformers, delivering unpleasant feedback, engaging in conflict, etc.).

So how does one become a better leader?

Again, there is no magic formula to leadership; the list of skills, competencies, and attitudes that a leader may be called upon to demonstrate is long and it is difficult to predict which will be necessary at any given time.

What follows is a framework for leadership development. We call this framework "Awareness to Action Leadership" because it is inspired by the Enneagram and some of the concepts from the book "Awareness to Action: The Enneagram, Emotional Intelligence, and Change" by Robert Tallon and Mario Sikora.

There is an old zen saying that if you want to become enlightened, you simply have to stand straight and breath. Doing so, however, requires years of effort and training. In the same way, good leadership begins with awareness and results in action, but there is a lifetime's worth of study and work that go into making one an Awareness to Action Leader.

We need to focus on the fundamentals—the broad concepts of leadership—all the time and also be able to dive down into focusing on very specific skills and competencies when necessary. The Awareness to Action Leadership framework can help us do that and is a useful guide for leaders and those who advise them.

In short, Awareness to Action Leadership:

- Starts with four broad questions.
- Identifies four simple leadership models that help to answer those questions.
- Provides a robust list of leadership competencies that are often required in leaders.
- Identifies a series of leadership stages that often determine which competencies are requisite.

Change often begins with asking the right questions. We encourage leaders to continually ask themselves these four:

- Am I continually working to improve my performance?
- Am I relating to others like a leader?
- Am I thinking the way a leader thinks?
- Am I preparing myself to scale (to take on larger challenges)?

We use four simple models to help our clients answer these questions.

The first model, which pertains to performance improvement or self-mastery, is the Awareness to Action process developed by Mario Sikora in the book "Awareness to Action." It has three sequential steps: increasing *awareness* of oneself and one's circumstances; rewriting one's story about the world to create *authenticity* or alignment between one's beliefs and one's goals; and taking deliberate, methodical *action* toward those goals.

Awareness, Authenticity, Action

The second model relates to the way a leader interacts with others.

At the heart of leadership is *power*—which is broadly defined as the capacity to produce an effect but which also includes things like responsibility for and control over the distribution of resources. It is important to acknowledge the role of power in leadership relationships; it's a topic that many people are uncomfortable with it. Ignoring the implications of power, however, pushes it into the shadow and leads to ineffective and inappropriate use. A good leader needs to be a student of power, understanding its implications, its nuance, and when to use how much of it.

Leadership Relationships

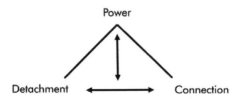

Power needs to be balanced by *connection* and *detachment,* two qualities that must exist in a dynamic tension with each other. Leaders must have the ability to connect to others and, simultaneously, to remain emotionally unattached. Without the ability to connect, a leader won't have followers; without the ability to remain detached, a leader won't be able to make the difficult, dispassionate decisions often required in positions of authority. Connection and detachment must exist in a dynamic tension with each other while the application of power lessens and intensifies based on the circumstances.

The third model relates to the way leaders should think. Like power is to leadership relationships, *rigor* is to leadership thinking. Leaders do not need to be the smartest person in the room, but they need to be committed to rigorous, critical thinking and good judgment. It is their responsibility to question, probe, and challenge information that is presented to them. The leader has no one else to blame if mistakes occur because no one took the time to ask the right questions. Of course, leaders must also use discretion on how aggressively to challenge data; their time is limited and they can't obsess over the details of every decision. A general rule is that greater potential consequences require greater rigor; matters of lesser consequence require less rigor; a request to spend $1 million deserves more rigor than a request to spend $1,000.

Rigor must be balanced by *curiosity* and *creativity*. In this context, curiosity is a broad hunger for knowledge and experience that may have no clear, immediate benefit other than being innately interesting. The great management thinker Peter Drucker always referred to management as a liberal art; I believe that great leaders think like liberal arts majors—wanting to know a little bit of something about everything. This curiosity must exist in a dynamic tension with creativity, however, which here refers to the *desire to bring something into being* (in addition to doing so in new and unique ways). Too much curiosity means that nothing gets done; too much creativity in this sense means that what gets done is not very useful. Without rigor, the leader won't know if the right thing is getting done or whether it is getting done correctly.

Leadership Thinking

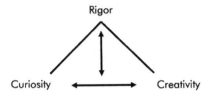

Fundamental to being in business is the need to grow the business, especially in a publicly traded company. Thus, in addition to asking "How do we grow the business?" a leader must be asking, "Am I able to grow *with* the business (i.e., am I able to scale to larger roles and greater responsibilities)?"

As I've already said, the factors that affect leadership performance are many. However, over the years of coaching leaders in a variety of organizations I have found that three fundamental competencies are critical to a leader's ability to rise through the ranks and assume greater responsibility: *creating processes and structures*; *developing talent and an effective network*; and *appropriately promoting oneself.*

The Scalable Leader

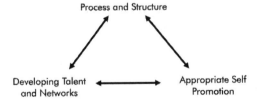

Every leader's daily life is a whirlwind—the best leaders find a way to minimize the chaos created by the whirlwind. The do this by creating as much **process and structure** as they can.

They create processes for routine activities so those activities become automatically attended. An ad hoc approach to routine tasks (treating them as unique occurrences each time they occur) wastes time and energy. Good leaders constantly evaluate how they spend their time and automate whenever possible.

They set goals but then rely on leading measures. They know what behaviors will lead to the accomplishment of their goal, and they focus on those actions. If they know that contact with their customer leads to high customer-satisfaction scores, for example, they focus on raising the incidents of contact rather than obsessing over the scores.

Developing others into strong individual performers, leaders, and a coherent team ensures that a leader can work at the right level, doing more-strategic work rather than having to do lower-level work to cover for weak subordinates. (To help my clients understand the significance of this I always tell them that if they are working at the wrong level they are being overpaid and should request a pay cut.)

Building and leveraging an effective network increases capacity because it expands one's range of available resources. In short, a leader with a broad network knows who to go to in order to get things done. They get more done faster.

Appropriate self-promotion means that one is more likely to be noticed and assigned larger roles. However, this is the competency that many of my clients find to be the most uncomfortable to work on—no one wants to be *that* person who gets ahead through self-promotion rather than ability. Thus, I encourage people to look at this issue from a business perspective rather than a "personal-gain" perspective. At a fundamental level, it is the responsibility of everyone in an organization to let people know what they are capable of. A leader (or anyone else) in an organization who has unrecognized skills or abilities is an underutilized resource. Leaders have a fiduciary responsibility to the company to help make full use of the resources; thus, it is incumbent upon every leader to give an accurate account of what they have accomplished and what they are capable of. In short, if a rising leader does not *promote themselves* they will stop rising to higher levels of responsibility and have less opportunity to help the company succeed.

These four heuristics or models are useful for leaders to keep in their mind. They also provide a skeleton on which to hang a lengthy list of more-specific skills, attitudes, or behaviors that make leaders more effective. Space does not allow me to go into to detailed explanations of each of these competencies or explanations of how to improve in them, but they are included in this guidebook for illustration. (See Tables 1-4 in the appendix of Awareness to Action coaching guidebook, which is available to ATAI clients.)

Finally, it is important to understand how the leadership level or tier may influence what competencies one should focus on. Again, there are many ways to think about this but we break them down into levels of responsibility and in terms of *direct*, *indirect*, or *strategic* leadership. *Direct leadership* is more hands-on and active, *indirect leadership* is less hands-on and more influence-based, and *strategic leadership* is more focused on setting direction and inspiring others. It is important to note that effective leaders practice elements of direct, indirect, and strategic leadership at all levels, but the leadership tier one is acting in determines where the preponderance of one's leadership approach should be focused.

The leadership tiers are:

- Manager of Individuals (Direct Leadership)
- Manager of Managers (transitioning from Direct to Indirect Leadership)
- Manager of a Function (Indirect Leadership)
- General manager of a business unit (transitioning from Indirect Leadership to Strategic Leadership)

- CEO (Strategic Leadership)

Table 5 in the appendix of the guidebook provides a guide to what competencies are most critical at which level. Again, this list is not meant to be exhaustive, and their placement on the various tiers is not iron-clad. As a leader, one must get good at worrying about what one needs to worry about and not worry about the rest. The Awareness to Action Leadership framework provides a useful checklist when thinking about what one should worry about, thus providing a useful starting point for ongoing leadership development. Most high-performing leaders first work to master the competencies required for their current level of responsibility and then seek to develop the competencies for the next level before they get there. You'll never get fired for being ahead of the leadership learning curve.

In summary, Awareness to Action Leadership provides a framework for leadership development; a guide both for leaders and for those who advise them. Leadership is more art than science, and no rules or models are absolute and complete in themselves. However, starting with the four big questions then burrowing down to more specific competencies provides a structured rather than haphazard approach to leadership development. Cross-matrixing those competencies with the five leadership tiers helps leaders prioritize their development in the absence of any specific situational demands.

About the Enneagram (And How It Can Help You)

People with all sorts of personalities can be successful at work. There are successful introverts and successful extroverts, successful optimists and successful pessimists. Our personality style doesn't determine our success, but while it is often the source of many of our strengths, it can create blind spots and obstacles that can hold us back.

The value of personality models is that they give us a framework for leveraging strengths and more-quickly recognizing blind spots and obstacles. A good model can also provide us with roadmaps for overcoming those blind spots and obstacles.

No model of personality styles does those things better than the Enneagram. This article gives an overview of the Enneagram model, which we use extensively at Awareness to Action International in our executive coaching and team building programs and which is at the heart of our "Personalities at Work" program. (See a short video about our "Personalities at Work" program www.ATAIVideos.com.)

Over the course of my 20 years as an executive coach and consultant I've encountered a lot of personality models; none of them come close to the Enneagram in terms of real-world applicability and usefulness. That is why it has become such a central part of my work—it helps get the results my clients expect.

"Enneagram" literally refers to a diagram with nine intersecting lines creating nine points enclosed in a circle ("ennea" is Greek for nine, "gram" for drawing). This diagram is used to represent nine personality styles and the interrelationships among those styles.

STRATEGY

INSTINCTUAL BIAS

There are two dimensions of personality described by the Enneagram. The first is our inherent system of instinctual values—what we habitually focus our attention on and what is important to us. The second dimension is the strategies we use to satisfy those values. In other words, the Enneagram helps us understand what is important to people and how they go about getting those things that are important to them.

(Note: Most approaches to the Enneagram focus more on the nine strategies—thus the "ennea"—and view the instinctual values as a secondary matter. At Awareness to Action International we understand that both dimensions are important and focus equally on both of them.)

Before we explain each of these dimensions further, we should take a moment to understand a bit about the way the mind works.

The brain requires an amount of energy that is far out of proportion to its mass. That three pounds or so between your ears requires about 20% of your energy expenditure. In order to minimize the amount of energy it expends, the brain has evolved ways to make our lives easier. One important way it does this is by habituating behavior—taking behaviors that work well and making them automatic—and by relying on patterns of behavior that can be repeated in as many situations as possible. This is why we have personality "styles"—they are one of the brain's techniques for applying the same pattern to multiple situations in an effort to save energy and increase efficiency.

Thus, when we talk about dimensions of personality styles we are talking about habitual patterns that, somewhere in the past, some part of our brains decided were effective. There is nothing wrong with having habits—they can be very effective in helping us get through life without having to face every situation as if for the first time. But we can also find ourselves falling into behavioral patterns that worked in the past but might not be quite right for a particular situation we face today, sometimes even causing more harm than good. Working with the Enneagram helps us recognize when we are using outdated or ill-suited patterns and it helps us develop the flexibility to free ourselves from them.

Dimension 1: Three Instinctual Biases

Dimension 1 of the Enneagram personality model is the three instinctual biases. The instinctual biases are deeply ingrained tendencies to find certain aspects of life more important than others and to focus our attention accordingly. These instinctual concerns fall into three broad domains. We all pay some attention to each of these domains, but we tend to focus on them unequally and we are biased toward one of the domains noticeably more than the others.

Those domains are:

- Preserving: focused on "nesting and nurturing" and on ensuring that fundamental survival needs are met for things like food, water, clothing, shelter, and overall safety from harm.

- Navigating: focused on "orienting to the group" and on building alliances, creating trust and reciprocity, and understanding how oneself and others fit into the group.

- Transmitting: focused on "attracting and bonding" and on passing genes, beliefs, values, interests, and worldview to others in order to make them carriers of that information.

What we value influences what we focus on at work. These instinctual biases have a dramatic effect on how we interact with coworkers, how we lead, how teams function, and more. (See the article "Instinctual

Leadership" in this collection for more on strengths and weaknesses of the instinctual biases.) People of different instinctual biases will focus on different tasks and objectives and we are often surprised when people place their priorities somewhere other than where we do. Such value discrepancies often a significant source of miscommunication and conflict in the workplace. Understanding the influence of the instinctual biases can help us reduce them.

Dimension 2: The Nine Strategies

There are nine distinct adaptive strategies for satisfying our instinctual concerns (again, the "Ennea" in "Enneagram" means nine). The strategies are consistent patterns of feeling, thinking, and doing that influence our interactions with the world around us (and the people in it). As with the instinctual domains, we use each of the nine strategies to a greater or lesser degree, but we use one of them more than the others. Because of the habitual overuse, we call this the "preferred" strategy. Each point on the Enneagram drawing represents one of these strategies.

In Enneagram parlance, the different personality styles are referred to by the number at which their preferred strategy is placed. Thus, someone whose preferred strategy is "striving to feel perfect" is referred to as an Ennea-type One; someone "striving to feel connected" is an Ennea-type Two, etc. (See Table 1 below for a very brief overview of the nine strategies.)

When we combine the instinctual biases with the preferred strategies we get three distinct versions of each Ennea-type. For example, an Ennea-type Three has a preferred strategy of "striving to feel outstanding," but a "Preserving Three" will non-consciously emphasize feeling outstanding in the preserving domain while a "Navigating Three" will emphasize feeling outstanding in the navigating domain.

It might seem simple, but understanding both dimensions provides profound insights into our own fundamental motivations and tendencies and those of the people we work with.

Because of its combination of simplicity and depth, the Enneagram is at the heart of many of our programs at Awareness to Action International.

We use it to help our executive coaching clients understand the self-imposed obstacles that can impede their personal effectiveness and to help remove those obstacles and develop new skills and competencies.

We use it in our Awareness to Action Teams program, helping team members not only see themselves more clearly but develop a better understanding what drives and motivates others, greatly enhancing their ability to communicate and collaborate.

We also use the Enneagram in our signature program, "Personalities at Work," a comprehensive introduction to the Enneagram and how it can be beneficial for individual contributors, managers, or senior leaders, helping to resolve conflict, improve communication, and enhance team collaboration and efficiency.

You can find out more about our programs in the short videos at www.ATAIPrograms.com or at www.AwarenessToAction.com.

Contact us today to find out more about how we can help you move from Awareness to Action through the use of the Enneagram model of personality styles. We have associates throughout the world who can deliver our programs or help you customize a solution that meets your specific needs.

Table 1: The Nine Ennea-Type Strategies

Ennea-Type One: Striving to Feel Perfect

They are often models of decorum, clear logic and appropriate behavior. They focus on rules, procedures and making sure that they are always doing the "right thing." When they overdo their Striving to be Perfect they can become critical, judgmental and unwilling to take risks. Under stress, Ones may fear that if they have too much fun they will become irresponsible.

Ennea-Type Two: Striving to Feel Connected

They are often selfless, caring and nurturing. They focus on helping others meet their needs; they build rapport easily and enjoy finding a common bond with others. When they overdo their Striving to be Connected they may fail to take care of their own needs and end up becoming emotionally dependent on others. Under stress, Twos may fear that if they are not closely connected to others they will become isolated.

Ennea-type Three: Striving to Feel Outstanding

They work hard to exceed standards and to be successful in whatever they undertake. They place high value on productivity and presenting an image of being a winner in whatever environment they are in. When they overdo their Striving to be Outstanding they may become attention seeking and may value image over substance. When stressed, Threes may fear that if they are not making great efforts to be excellent they will become mediocre.

Ennea-Type Four: Striving to Feel Unique

They generally approach their lives creatively, in fresh and interesting ways. They gravitate toward things and experiences that are elegant, refined, or unusual. When they overdo their Striving to be Unique they may feel misunderstood, and they may withdraw from others and become isolated. When stressed, Fours may fear that if they do not put their own special touch on their world and their experiences their individuality will become repressed.

Ennea-type Five: Striving to Feel Detached

They are observant, logical and generally reserved. They focus on problem solving, innovative ideas, and data gathering. When they overdo their Striving to be Detached they can end up being dull—out of touch with their experiences and emotions. When stressed, Fives may fear that if they do not remain detached and guarded they will become uncontrolled.

Ennea-Type Six: Striving to Feel Secure

They find security in being part of something bigger than themselves, such as a group or tradition. They are careful, responsible and protective of the welfare of the group. They focus on maintaining consistency, tradition and cohesion. When they overdo their Striving to be Secure they may fail to take the risks necessary for high performance and settle for mediocrity. When stressed, Sixes may fear that if they relax their guard they will be vulnerable to possible dangers.

Ennea-Type Seven: Striving to Feel Excited

They are upbeat, enthusiastic, optimistic, and curious. They focus on possibilities and options and keeping others entertained. When they overdo their Striving to be Excited they may fail to follow-through, become easily distracted, and act irresponsibly. When stressed, Sevens may fear that if they do not fill their heads with many thoughts they will miss out on something.

Ennea-Type Eight: Striving to Feel Powerful

They are action-oriented self-starters who love to be in charge. They focus on getting things done and overcoming obstacles that may lie in their way. When they overdo their Striving to be Powerful they may not adhere to the rules or norms that others expect them to follow and their behavior can become uncontrolled. When stressed, Eights may fear that if they become too connected to others or experience their own emotions too deeply they will become dependent on others.

Ennea-Type Nine: Striving to Feel Peaceful

They are calm, pleasant, and charming. They focus on maintaining a sense of inner harmony by minimizing their own needs and concentrating on the needs of others. When they overdo their Striving to be Peaceful they can become passive, relying on others to make decisions for them. When stressed, Nines may fear that if they place too much importance on themselves they will be seen as attention seeking.

Instinctual Leadership

Each of us is wired with instinctual drives that shape what we value and what aspects of life we focus on. These drives have been wired into us through millions of years of evolutionary pressures and they enhance our ability to survive and reproduce. Understanding how these instinctual drives influence our work lives has a transformative effect.

These drives can be thought of as fitting into three distinct domains—Preserving, Navigating, and Transmitting—and while we each exhibit behaviors related to all three domains, we tend to have a non-conscious bias toward one of them. Some of us focus more on Preserving, some on Navigating, and some on Transmitting. This focus can be the source of our greatest strengths and our most significant blind spots

"Instinctual Leadership" is a way of understanding how these instinctual drives affect our work lives—the way we work, the way we lead, and the way we function in teams—and leveraging that understanding for positive change. It combines a model of the three instinctual biases with a model of nine strategies for satisfying the values and addressing the issues our biases compel us toward.

This combination of instinctual biases and strategies is a specific approach to the Enneagram model of personality styles. The article will focus on the three instinctual biases, but the table below lists the nine strategies as a reminder for those already familiar with the Enneagram system. For those not familiar with the model, please refer to www.EnneagramVideos.com or "Awareness to Action: The Enneagram, Emotional Intelligence, and Change" by Robert Tallon and Mario Sikora.

TABLE 1: The Nine Ennea-Types

Ennea-Type:	Preferred Strategy:
One	Striving to be Perfect
Two	Striving to be Connected
Three	Striving to be Outstanding
Four	Striving to be Unique
Five	Striving to be Detached
Six	Striving to be Secure
Seven	Striving to be Excited
Eight	Striving to be Powerful
Nine	Striving to be Peaceful

The Three Instinctual Domains

The *Preserving* domain is a group of instinctual impulses that relates to nesting and nurturing needs. They are inclinations to ensure we have the resources we need to survive, to ensure that we are safe and secure, to ensure shelter and comfort. In addition to these fundamental "self"-preservation needs, however, this domain also includes preservation of artifacts, traditions, our offspring, and those people we hold dear. It is an innate desire to ensure not only that we survive, but that those who carry our genes survive and prosper, and that we have the resources necessary to ensure that survival.

The instinctual drives in the *Navigating* domain help us navigate or orient to the group. They help us understand group dynamics, social status, and cultural mores and they equip us with skills that enable us to know who we can trust and develop reciprocal relationships with. As social creatures we need to understand how the group works and how to be accepted into it. We have to gather information about others but only reveal enough about ourselves to maintain a favorable reputation. We need to know who is in "the tribe" and who is not, and how we can ensure we remain a part of the social security network. The navigating behaviors help us do that.

The Transmitting domain of instinctual drives enhances the likelihood that we will attract the attention of others and it equips us to demonstrate the value of our ideas, values, creations, or genes. This domain is about attention and intensity; it is about display and enticement. Commonly thought of as being focused on one-to-one relationships, it is more accurate to say that this group of instinctual behaviors enhances our ability to make sure some part of ourselves passes on to the next generation.

It can be helpful to see the instinctual biases as an independent, but limited, typology. For example, people who are Preserving types will share some characteristics with other people who are Preserving types regardless of their Enneagram type. But, as with the Ennea-types, we must be careful about oversimplifying human nature and making too many assumptions about how the instinctual behaviors will manifest in any given individual. Some Preservers take a minimalist approach to maintaining resources, keeping on hand only what they need, while others will warehouse an overabundance of resources. What they share is an instinctual focus on preservation, even if they manifest those instincts in different ways.

Further, people often contradict themselves in the instinctual domains; Preservers will pinch pennies one moment but extravagantly indulge their desires the next.

This is probably due to two factors:

- The modular nature of the brain—different mechanisms have evolved over time that support the same need but do so in conflicting ways; both conservation of resources and indulgence support one's well-being under different circumstances.

- The fact that we have evolved to both compete and cooperate; frequently with the same people at the same time. We have to compete AND cooperate with family members, team members, vendors, and—sometimes—even competitors, and we put the instinctual behaviors to use in doing so.

These contradictions can be confusing, but if we understand the root of the conflicts and that they ultimately serve the same end, they become easier to work with.

Finally, when it comes to drawing distinctions within the instinctual domains, it helps to remember that different Ennea-types will express the instinctual biases differently. For example, while a Transmitting Nine and a Transmitting Eight will share some fundamental values (namely, a desire to "transmit"), their different adaptive strategies will cause them to satisfy their values in different ways. A Transmitting Nine and a Transmitting Eight may look similar in some behaviors and attitudes but they will be very different in others. The same applies to other Ennea-types as well; people will have similarities when they share a strategy and instinctual bias, but behave differently where strategy and instinctual bias differences exist.

Leadership

Our character expresses itself in all areas of our life, and *how* we lead is often an outcome of *who* we are. Our leadership style can't help but be influenced by our Ennea-type—Eights tend to be more directive leaders while Nines tend to be more consensus-building in their approach, for example—and our instinctual bias shapes our leadership as well.

The scope of this article does not allow us to go into great depth, but the following are some observations I've made over nearly two decades of working with leaders. I want to emphasize again that the Enneagram should not be used as a predictive model; it should be used as a remedial model or a model to make one aware of probabilities. When I work with a client, I can't assume that because they are a Navigating type they will *definitely* exhibit a particular behavior, but I can use the model to help me watch out for particular tendencies and as a guide for helping the client change ineffective behavior.

I have also observed that there is a particular pattern related to the expression of the instinctual biases that affects leadership. It seems that one domain is dominant and often "over-attended to;" one domain is paid some attention but often in a conflicted way; and one domain is relatively ignored until circumstances force our attention to it. My observation has been that the expression of the domain-related behaviors tends to be consistent so if you know which domain is dominant you will know which one is secondary and which is tertiary. The ordering of expression seems to be in the following patterns:

- Preserving dominant—Navigating secondary— Transmitting tertiary.

- Navigating dominant—Transmitting secondary— Preserving tertiary.

- Transmitting dominant—Preserving secondary— Navigating tertiary.

Understanding this pattern can be very useful because it tells us not only where a client may be over-using their instinctual behaviors, but also what important instinctual behaviors are probably being neglected. For example, if a leader is a Preserving type there is a very good chance that he or she is not only overly focused on preserving behaviors but that he or she is probably neglecting the necessary transmitting behaviors of leadership and conflicted in the navigating domain.

Preserving Leaders:

The Preserving domain of instinctual behaviors is related to the preservation of resources and the well-being of oneself and the people in the proverbial nest. Those people may well include co-workers and subordinates, and Preservers often spend a lot of time thinking about their own security and the security of those for whom they are responsible. Note that they may not be effective at ensuring that security, but it will be a disproportionate concern for them. I have known Preserving types who fixate on having enough of the things they need but still being reckless with their finances in ways that undermine their security; others who focus so much on preserving their resources that they are too stingy in the appropriate use of those resources. The commonality is the amount of time and energy spent focused on preserving-related issues even if they express the focus via different behaviors.

Therefore, I will write about what each instinctual type is "drawn to"— i.e., where their attention and focus goes—with the acknowledgement that they may not be effective at actually doing those things or even find pleasure in doing them.

Preserving-type leaders tend to be drawn to the fundamental, "nuts and bolts" issues related to business and organizations. They tend to be more cautious and conservative, and more risk-averse in general. They tend to want to ensure that administrative issues are in order and that procedures are being followed. They can be circumspect and cautious about change and new ways of doing things, and they often like to be the Devil's Advocate who challenges new ideas. They often prefer tradition to experimentation, but they can also bring strong process focus to an effort and drive deliberate change through disciplined execution. These tendencies can make them good leaders for organizations that need stability and order. The downside is that they can be too resistant to change, conservative, and tradition-bound and may struggle in a fast-changing environment where the objective is not clearly defined.

Preserving Leaders are:

- Good at preserving the "nest": ensuring their own security and the security of co-workers and subordinates they are responsible for.

- Good at playing Devil's advocate and challenging ideas that may not be fully thought-through. However, can be risk-averse, resistant to change and new ways of doing things.

- Good at ensuring that administrative issues are in order and that procedures are being implemented and followed.

- Comfortable in organizations that need stability and order; they may struggle in a fast changing environment.

- May be too introverted: focus on tasks rather than interpersonal issues.

- May lack charisma; can seem detached rather than inspirational.

Navigating Leaders:

The Navigating domain of instinctual concerns is related to issues of trust, reciprocity, and identity within the group. These behaviors help us know what our status is within the hierarchy, how to build collaborative relationships with others, and how to navigate the politics of the group. Navigating types are generally interested in the exchange of information—seeking insights about people and sharing gossip. They want to track the actions of those within the group, thus they like to be around people even if they don't engage with others. They are sociable, but also somewhat guarded—revealing enough to be accepted but not so much that they will be rejected. At times, they may come across to others as gossipy, overly political or position-conscious, and not taking a clear stand on an issue.

Navigating leaders are drawn to issues related to group dynamics and interpersonal communication. They track group cohesion and status changes; they tend to be attuned to organizational politics, intuitively knowing which levers to pull in order to move projects around obstacles. They are able to instinctively read the pulse of the group, assess morale, and know who needs to be pushed, who needs to be nurtured, and who the influencers are. They tend to be good at identify the needs of the various constituencies in the organization and finding ways to satisfy them. Navigating leaders tend to be good in the "forming" stage of team dynamics, where the group is finding its identity and ways of working together. They may, however, become too focused on the political dynamics of the group and spend more time on the politics than on the organization's ultimate business goals.

Navigating Leaders are:

- Naturally drawn to issues related to group dynamics and interpersonal communication.

- Track group cohesion and status changes.

- Attuned to organizational politics, intuitively knowing which levers to pull in order to move projects around obstacles.

- Ability to instinctively read the pulse of the group, build the consensus, and know who needs to be pushed, who need to be nurtured, and who the influencers are.

- Good at the "forming" stage of team dynamics, where the group is finding its identity and ways of working together.

- Good at big picture and strategic thinking.

- Can be too focused on the political dynamics of the group, spending more time on the politics than on the organization's ultimate business goal.

- May have poor administrative capabilities.

- Less comfortable in difficult individual interaction and personnel decisions (e.g. addressing underperformance, firing, reprimanding).

Transmitting Leaders:

The Transmitting domain of instincts is related to displaying the desirability of the individual and his or her ideas or creations. These instinctual behaviors help us attract the attention of others, seduce them into seeing our desirability or the desirability of our creations. Transmitters know how to stand out and draw attention, to charm and cajole, to create an intense connection that induces the other to be open to what the Transmitter has to offer. Transmitters tend to be engaging and intuitively understand how to entice others into their orbit. They are typically ambitious and apparently self-confident, and they can be willing to take risks to get what they want.

Transmitting leaders are often charismatic and bold. They are often good at articulating a goal or vision and moving others toward it, seducing some and driving others as necessary. They often intuitively understand the mind of the market and the customer and are persuasive sellers of the product, company, or dream. They can be competitive and are often the alpha males and females of the group. Transmitting leaders tend to be good in the start-up phase of a business when the organization needs an inspiring vision to rally around. On the downside, the transmitting behaviors can cause these leaders to focus too much on themselves, their accomplishments, and their desirable qualities, making them seem overly self-centered.

Transmitting Leaders are:

- Often charismatic and bold.

- Good at articulating a goal or vision and moving others toward it, seducing some and driving others as necessary.

- Intuitively understand the mind of the market and the customer; persuasive seller of the products, company or dream.

- Good at building relationships with customers, channel partners and strategic allies.

- Highly competitive (alpha male or female of the group).

- Good at the start-up phase of a business, when the workforce needs an inspiring vision to rally around.

- May place too much focus on themselves, their accomplishments and their desirable qualities. May neglect career development of subordinates.

- Self-focus may seem to put own interests before company/employees.

Secondary and Tertiary Domains:

Because of the predictable order of the instincts, we also have clues for what to look for regarding the leader's secondary and tertiary instinctual domains.

Preserving leaders, for example, often neglect the leadership behaviors related to their third instinctual domain—those very leadership capabilities that are typically the strengths of the Transmitting leaders. They tend to be understated and conservative, focused on process to the neglect of inspiration. They may neglect the "selling" component of leadership, failing to focus enough on marketing and sales or the selling of the vision. They are often ambivalent and conflicted about the needs addressed by the Navigating domain—they have some tolerance for the organizational politics but see it as a diversion from more-important tasks; they may understand the value of "management by walking around" or talking with people to gauge the emotional temperature of the team but they frequently find reasons to neglect doing so.

Navigating leaders frequently neglect those activities addressed by their tertiary instinctual domain—the Preserving behaviors. They may fail to appropriately value or follow process, overlook threats to the company's competitive position, and ignore details that could be the signs of bigger problems. As in Aesop's fable, they can be the grasshopper who wants to chat and enjoy the sunshine with the ant rather than the preserving ant who is preparing for the winter. They are often conflicted in the leadership behaviors of the Transmitting domain. They may want to shine, but are hesitant to draw too much attention to their gifts; they may want to drive a vision, but worry too much about the political impacts of doing so.

Transmitting leaders, though seeming outgoing and "social," typically neglect the leadership duties supported by the Navigating behaviors. They have little time for gossip or organizational politics beyond what it takes to advance their agenda. Their social interactions are usually transactional and have a definite purpose—to charm and sell their ideas when necessary—but they are not usually great listeners and quickly grow weary of social small talk. They are conflicted in the Preserving domain—they want to accumulate the resources necessary to meet their goals and they want to be comfortable and pampered, but they can be reckless—sometimes reaching for the whole pie rather than only the amount they need. They may forget to be appropriately conservative when conservatism is called for.

Again, it is important to point out that while these descriptions are useful, they point to broad tendencies and there are many subtleties that can be addressed if we were to look at the 27 subtypes, which are the result of the interaction of the three instinctual biases and the nine strategies. A Navigating One may be more detail-oriented than a Navigating Nine, for example, but they are not nearly as detail-oriented as a Preserving One or even a Preserving Three. Transmitting Fives aren't typically as charismatic and outgoing as Transmitting Sevens, but they can be more extroverted and energetic than many Preserving Nines or Preserving Fours.

In conclusion, we have to be careful when making assumptions about broad groups of people, whether we are looking only at the three instinctual biases or the nine Ennea-types. However, it is clear that accurately identifying a leader's instinctual bias can help him or her develop important and vivid insights into their nature and the nature of their leadership. Combining this with an understanding of each Ennea-type's strategy makes the value even greater. It is my hope that leaders and those that work with them can use this article as a starting pointing point for further exploration and growth.

System 1, System 2, and the Nine Strategies: Blending Insights from Modern Cognitive Psychology with the Enneagram

Daniel Kahneman's book "Thinking Fast and Slow" has helped popularize the idea that we have two general cognitive systems for processing information. Kahneman's book is one of many popular volumes published in recent years that describe what we have learned from the cognitive sciences over the past few decades about the workings of the mind. These insights can provide very useful insights in how to use the Enneagram to create change.

System 1, as Kahneman describes, is fast, heuristic-based thinking. It relies on deeply rooted mental models that allow us to make quick decisions without having to think any more than absolutely necessary, if we think at all. The beauty of System 1 is that it is generally good enough to help us meet the basic demands of daily life without requiring us to expend too much energy. Unfortunately, it is not always accurate. While it is often very effective for solving short-term problems, it can cause us to act in ways that undermine us in the long run.

System 2 is slow, rational thinking. It is the conscious, deliberate weighing of variables and data and considering of long-term consequences. It is more accurate, but it also requires more caloric energy and is physically demanding, so we tend to minimize its use. (Ever notice how tired you are after a long period of concentrated thinking or attention? This is the result of System 2 causing the brain to burn a lot of energy.)

Broadly, the existence of these two systems means that we have access to two thinking modes that both serve a useful end, but we sometimes use one when we should use the other–with unfortunate results. For example, we may come to regret relying on System 2 slow thinking when we accidentally step out into traffic or relying on System 1 fast thinking when deciding to buy a used car.

Understanding that there are two systems and when we tend to use each can be a big help in our personal development. Our lives become more efficacious when we use each system appropriately, allowing ourselves to conserve energy and mental resources by delegating mundane activities to System 1 but using System 2 when a circumstance is more fluid or complex. In fact, with practice we can use System 2 to reconfigure certain heuristics in System 1 as more-effective habits. This is how we develop virtue–by consciously practicing virtuous behaviors until they become habit and we do them automatically.

Most of our habitual patterns are the result of processes created in System 1, and these include the habitual pattern related to our Ennea-type. Through repetition that starts very early in life, we develop reactions to the world that are based on one of nine adaptive strategies. The preferred strategy is, in a sense, one of System 1's heuristics and we can end up using the strategy in effective ways or ineffective ways. The key to growth with this approach to the Enneagram is understanding when we are using the strategy ineffectively in System 1 and then deliberately using System 2 to help us either get rid of the maladaptive behavior or redefine the strategy in such a way that System 1 will use it effectively in the future.

There are some who would argue that we should strive for a state of constant awareness, which would mean living in a version of System 2 all the time. Modern cognitive science shows us why this aspiration is not realistic (and probably why no one can actually do it)–System 2 simply requires too much energy. Prolonged conscious awareness, to the extent that it is possible, is exhausting.

A more realistic approach is to apply the Awareness to Action Process to use System 2 to challenge the implicit assumptions of our preferred strategy, rewrite the strategy in a more-adaptive way, and then practice adaptive or virtuous behaviors aligned with the new mindset so it becomes a habitual part of our System 1 thinking. (See the article, " The Missing Piece in Creating Change" in this collection.)

For example, the adaptive strategy of Ennea-type Nine is "striving to feel peaceful." Their System 1, habitual and heuristic-based thinking, causes them to avoid anything that seems like self-praise or high self-regard (such behaviors may potentially cause conflict if the egos of others feel threatened). They habitually self-deprecate–subtly put themselves down and deflect praise from others. While this often makes them seem like humble, likable people, it can hold them back professionally because people start to believe their self-deprecations are reality. Further, they become resentful when, as an outcome of this automatic behavior, they are not recognized for their contributions.

Nines need to step into System 2 and re-evaluate their implicit beliefs about what it means to feel "peaceful" and to realize that they can achieve more inner contentment by self-deprecating less often. With practice, System 1 adopts the new behavior and System 2 can focus on something else, if necessary, or just take a break.

Growth–whether it be personal, professional, or spiritual–does not require being fully aware all of the time, even if such a thing was possible. It requires being aware of the right things at the right time. It is based on having the skills to recognize when one needs to think, act, or feel differently than one is at the moment. It requires having the skills and willingness to use System 2 slow thinking to challenge our assumptions and recognize when System 1 fast thinking fails us. It includes being able to switch from System 1 to System 2 at the appropriate times, and to develop virtuous or adaptive habits so we can allow both systems to do their job.

The Missing Piece in Creating Change

Most advice on how to change is very straightforward (and simplistic): Become aware of your patterns and what you need to do differently, then make a plan for doing the new behavior. Of course, if it were that easy, everyone would keep their New Year's resolutions and the whole self-help industry would fade into irrelevance. Executive coaches like me would have to get real jobs...

We all know that change is not easy. The reason that most attempts to change fail is because they overlook a critical step between "become aware" and "act in a new way"–they fail to resolve the internal conflicts created by the attempt to change.

As Robert Kegan and Lisa Laskow Lahey point out it their work on immunity to change, attempts to change create competing commitments in our psyche. Intellectually, we know we should change and that the change would be good for us, but we also have an old narrative that tells us that what we are currently doing is *also* good for us in some way. The old behavior has the advantage of being comfortable and familiar, while the intended change is new and its value is not yet proven. Our internal narrative is that the old behavior has been effective, and changing will make us less effective in some way. The change we wish to make often seems to be in conflict with our narrative, and thus seems illogical. When we attempt to change, we face a conflict: we want to change but, deep down, the change doesn't really make sense to us.

Kegan and Lahey point out that rewriting our narrative in a way that honors the existing commitment *and* the new commitment is the only way to overcome the inner conflict that causes our immunity to change. The beauty of the Enneagram model of personality styles is that it tells us exactly what those narratives are based on–nine adaptive strategies and our habitual definitions of them–making it easier to rewrite them.

Before exploring this further, let's back up see how these narratives take root.

Fortunately, we humans have a great ability to function on autopilot. Life is complicated, filled with mundane tasks as well as complex activities that require our attention. In order to have time to think about the complex issues, we have evolved the ability to "outsource" the mundane to our internal autopilot. How much could we get done if we really had to be fully conscious and present when we were tying our shoes or brushing our teeth in the morning, feeding the dog, and packing the kids' lunch, and didn't allow ourselves to think about when we have to pick up our children from school and which event to taxi them to in the evening, the project due at work, what bills need to be paid, how we will deal with the care of our aging parents, or any of the other myriad of concerns that require our attention more than our shoelaces? Much of the day, for many of the things we do, we just need to trust our autopilot.

But while there many benefits, there are also downsides to this ability to be on autopilot–we sometimes miss our exit on the highway because our minds are elsewhere, we are lost in thought and forget our briefcase, we leave our dry-cleaning at the pre-school and our preschooler at the dry-cleaners…

When we realize that we have made one of these blunders, we are filled with a moment of anxiety or uncertainty (or downright terror, in the case of the dry-cleaning and preschool), and we immediately seek to create a narrative that resolves the situation in our mind and allows us to go back to functioning on autopilot. We "wake up" on the highway and are not sure how we got to where we are, so we look for signs or landmarks that help us locate ourselves; we remind ourselves that we are busy and we'll find a way to function without the briefcase;

we blame our wife for assuming we could manage two things at once...
We eventually return to our zoned-out bliss, comfortable with our story.

So, how do we change?

The inertia of habituated behavior is strong; our habitual narratives give us a sense (often false) of order and direction. Our narratives create immunity to change, and attempts to change that violate the logic of our narratives are rejected the same way the body rejects a transplanted organ of the wrong blood type.

The only way to change behavior over the long term is to change the narrative. However, we can't simply abandon a narrative that has, in many ways, worked for us for much of our lives; we have to revise it so that it honors the past and our existing values while becoming more accurate given our current circumstances. We have to create a narrative that is more *authentic*.

The Enneagram can help us do just that, because it tells us what is at the core of our narratives–an adaptive strategy that shapes the way we think, feel, and behave. Unfortunately, that strategy is often defined in narrow and restricting ways; what was once adaptive can now be maladaptive. Attempts to change often conflict with the existing definition of the strategy and meet resistance. If we want to change, the only way we can make the narrative more authentic is to redefine our preferred strategy in more adaptive ways.

The steps to creating change are not simple "awareness" and "action;" if we want to change we must address the crucial middle step– "authenticity."

Let's look at an example.

One of the typical issues that my Ennea-type Three clients have to work on is their ability to develop and delegate to subordinates. Their preferred adaptive strategy is "striving to be outstanding." They have an affective need to *feel* like they are high-achieving and meeting the high expectations they set for themselves and have internalized from others. This affective need makes them *think* in ways that have to do with how outstanding they are and how they can be more outstanding. The way they think shapes the way they *behave* and they try to behave in ways that will make them feel more outstanding. This, of course, is not the only motivation of Threes, but it is a strong one.

A common theme for my Three clients is that they rose to their level of success by being outstanding "doers"–working harder and faster than others, demonstrating superior performance. They are the classic achievers that David McClelland wrote about–people driven to set goals and achieve them, to be admired by others, to fulfill (at minimum) the ideals of the community. Their habitual narrative is often rooted in an attachment to be seen as outstanding doer, and this can be their undoing as they rise to higher levels of leadership responsibility. Throughout their lives they have defined what it means to be "outstanding" as doing things better than other people. This narrow definition of the strategy has become calcified and rote. In their need to achieve they find it more satisfactory to do a task themselves rather than to take the time to teach others to do it and then delegate, even if this means that they end up with more and more work to do. The pattern becomes unsustainable as their responsibility grows and they can eventually burn out or fail to meet the commitments they have taken on.

It would be easy to say to these leaders, "Stop doing it yourself, develop your team and delegate to them." If you did give them that advice, they would nod their heads and agree that it makes sense. They might even try it for a while. But quickly the inner conflict will undermine their efforts because the new behavior seems to undermine their narrowly defined implicit strategy. They ask, How can I perform better than others or strive for high standards of accomplishment if I take time out to teach other people how to do something? I will probably just have to redo it anyway because the other person surely won't do it as well as I could have done it. Therefore, it just makes sense to do it myself.

Someone who does not have this same preferred strategy is working on a different model of logic and may easily see the flaws in this line of thinking. But each of us can get trapped by our narrative and be blind to what seems obvious to others.

In order to change, the Three leader must revise their narrative and rewrite the preferred strategy. In this case, they would recognize that their restrictive, calcified narrative is outdated and maladaptive and they would revise the strategy at its core to something along the lines of "Instead of being an outstanding doer, I will strive to be an outstanding leader. Outstanding leaders do the following things: develop people, delegate effectively so they can work at higher levels...."

If the Three can see that the change they want to make can help them actually *satisfy* a fundamental value (being outstanding), not undermine it. When the strategy is redefined and the narrative rewritten in such a way, I find that the client actually *wants* to make the change and undertakes the action plan eagerly. The conflict between the inner commitments is resolved.

Taken together, the Awareness to Action Process looks like this:

1. Awareness: Pay attention. Recognize your habitual patterns. Set a goal for change.

2. Authenticity: Identify the conflicting commitments created by the change. Rewrite your narrative by redefining the preferred strategy in a way that honors your values and makes the change attractive.

3. Action: Create a simple and specific action plan.
Deliberately practice the new behaviors to resist reverting back to old narratives.

4. *Repeat*!

While the missing piece of most change efforts is found in the "authenticity" step, we must also realize that this is an ongoing activity. We can't just rewrite the narrative once, since all narratives are limited and, by their nature, eventually become outdated. We should be constantly redefining the strategy—challenging our assumptions and dismantling our defenses and resistance, venturing farther from our traditional comfort zones. The word "authenticity" has the same root as the word "author." Being authentic in this case means taking control of our narratives and being the author of our own lives; writing a story that is more aligned with our current reality than our habituated past.

Rather than allowing our narratives and our implicit definition of our strategy to be calcified and bounded, we should constantly work on clarifying the definition of the strategy, making it permeable so that it gradually includes more and more possibilities. Sticking with the example of the Three Leader, constantly challenging and reshaping the implicit definition of striving to be outstanding eventually leads to a definition of outstanding that includes one who has given up on such strivings. This is the path to freedom from the grip of the calcified strategy.

Yes, our implicit limited and calcified definitions of the strategy are often used in ineffective or outdated ways; it is a lens that can easily become covered with mud and grime. But it is our nature to view life through some lens or adopt some strategy. It makes no sense to reinvent the wheel for each new circumstance; life is easier when we find a strategy that works for us and work on clarifying it.

But we must continually polish and clean the lens; the strategy must serve us rather than us becoming a slave to it. While the implicit strategy is bound and calcified, treating it like clay or dough to be kneaded and stretched allows it to become permeable and frees us to use other strategies without feeling like we have lost something we can't live without.

Over time, the strategy transforms from resembling a steel ring that restrains us to seeming like the expansive and fluid ripples on the surface of a pond. The *outstanding doer* becomes the *outstanding leader* as she understands that it is empowering others that leads to true greatness. She understands that the outstanding careerist can become the outstanding parent or spouse. It begins to take hold that the truly outstanding person is motivated by higher values than the perceptions and judgments of other people, and that the most outstanding person you can be is to simply be your authentic self.

Effective, lasting change begins with working with the preferred strategy–simultaneously challenging it, embracing it and reclaiming it from the shadow, redefining it in adaptive ways that serve us rather than restrict us. Ignoring the "authenticity" step in the Awareness to Action process is to miss the whole point and to set ourselves up for failure on the path to change.

*Kegan, Robert and Lisa Laskow Lahey, "Immunity to Change."

The Theatrics of Leadership

All the world's a stage,
And all the men and women merely players:
They have their exits and their entrances;
And one man in his time plays many parts
William Shakespeare, "As You Like It"

All the world is a stage, but we tend to observe it from the inside out rather than the outside in. That is, we tend to see the world and interpret it from our own perspective—our values, our judgments, our biases—and it can be difficult for us to see ourselves from the perspective of another.

This is even true of leaders—they tend to think they are *watching* the play when in reality they are the ones on stage. It is easy to forget this, and it is very easy to overlook the ramifications of not practicing what I call "the theatrics of leadership."

To illustrate the point: an analogy and a story.

First, the analogy. The Thanksgiving holiday is an important one in the US. It is common for families to gather for a big dinner, and often there are multiple generations joined together. The number of people usually exceeds the number of seats at the main table, and a second table is provided for the children. In my family, it was always referred to as "the kids' table." Eventually, we all grow up and move to the "grown-ups' table" but, psychologically, we feel like part of us still belongs at the kids table and we carry this feeling around with us our whole lives. No matter how much we accomplish and how old we are, we all have moments when we ask "When did I become the one carving the turkey?"

Now, the story: Jim Atkinson was the general manager of a large global business unit of a multinational corporation. He was responsible for almost $2bn of the company's revenue and the jobs of thousands of employees. He was smart, talented, energetic and professional. He was approachable, and he continually made it clear that he thought he was no better than anyone else. He was always telling people, "I'm nobody special, just call me Jim." He took pride in seeing himself as a regular guy. When he went home at night he tried to find the time to watch a ball game and have a beer. His children loved him but thought he was kind of a dork; his wife treated him well, but was quick to remind him that the garbage needed to be taken out and give him a hard time for forgetting to pick up milk on his way home.

What Jim didn't realize was that while he saw himself as "just Jim," the people who worked for him saw him as "Jim Atkinson," the Boss, a Very Important Person. They would sit up straighter when he was in the building. They walked a little faster and worked a little harder. Like cold-war era CIA Kremlin watchers, they would observe and analyze Jim, looking for clues that could tell them anything—how the company was doing, how the BU was doing, whether or not there would be a layoff, how he thought they were doing their jobs.

Jim had climbed the corporate ladder quickly and was barely 40 years old when he assumed the general manager position. He was doing okay, but there were some questions regarding his "executive presence" and I was asked to come in to coach him. "Executive presence" is a bit of a catch-all phrase, but with some digging it became clear that his desire to be "just Jim" was undermining people's confidence in him. He didn't realize that while he saw himself as a "regular person," others needed to see him as "Jim Atkinson," the Boss, a Very Important Person.

He sometimes forgot that people need a leader they can have confidence in; that the person who was carving the turkey would give them all their fair share, but also that he would carve it with competence and skill. They needed to credibly see him as the person who sat at the head of the table.

When Jim received the feedback we discussed the importance of remembering that he needed to *act the part* of the leader *as well as being* the leader. He had an initial fear that I wanted him to focus on style over substance, but I explained that substance was a given, that without substance none of it mattered, but that if he didn't appear to be the kind of leader that people needed to see, he would fail no matter how much substance he had. Thus, we started working on ways that he could be project more executive presence while still being true to his core values. I explained that when actors play a role they looked for something inside themselves that they could draw on to display the traits of the character they are inhabiting. The best of them were authentic even as they played a role. He didn't need to be forceful and "bossy" (unless circumstances specifically required that), but he needed to find the balance between friendly and commanding, approachable and self-contained, relaxed and purposeful.

Jim had great raw material and the fixes were relatively minor. The important part was to get beyond seeing the world through his spectator perspective and to realize that *he* was the one on stage and he needed to play to the audience. It didn't matter that he wanted to play the role of "Just Jim," he was hired to play "Jim Atkinson, the Boss" and if he didn't play the role the way the audience expected, he would lose them.

Getting Your Leadership Story Right

It's challenging in that we give up the security of comfortable patterns and familiar relationships.

It's exciting because it is usually for a bigger and better role that provides new opportunities to learn, be challenged, and work with new people.

It's also an opportunity to, if not necessarily reinvent, at least refresh the leader's personal "brand" or identity.

It's an opportunity that no leader should squander.

Consider Thomas, a classic success story by most measures. Thomas had been at a company for nearly 25 years. He joined the company as a laborer on a production line when he was 18 but through intelligence and drive he worked his way up to become general manager of one of the business verticals reporting to a segment president who reported to the CEO. In fact, he was often referred to as "the Wonder Kid" because of the precocious intelligence and business savvy he showed early in his career.

But Thomas wanted more—he was still young but was passed over twice for larger roles and he couldn't figure out why.

The problem was that even though he was no longer that 18-year old kid on the factory floor, there were still people who remembered him that way. While they respected him and Thomas was broadly acknowledged as being smarter and more effective than almost anyone around him, there were still too many people who remembered him as "the Kid." A perception had been anchored in the minds of just enough of the decision makers to keep him from going any further.

An opportunity came along for Thomas to move to a new company in a role similar to the one he was in. It was not a step up, necessarily, but it was an opportunity to rewrite the narrative about him—he would be going into his new company at a high level and that would be the perception people started with; the image of the kid on the factory floor would not be an issue.

Thomas, being as smart as he is, went into his new role with a 100-day plan* that included all of the things a new leader is supposed to do. But it also included an activity that most people overlook when they make transitions: he focused on what he wanted his leadership brand to be and he took steps to establish that brand.

The opportunity to rewrite one's leadership brand is something that doesn't come along that often, and it is not only something that failed leaders should do—even the best leaders carry some baggage from their past in their organizations they are in. Thus, this is an opportunity to refresh, if not necessarily reinvent.

Here are some steps to take to establish your leadership brand in a new company:

- *Before you go, take the opportunity to do a leadership best-practice analysis.* Who are the leaders you admire? What qualities do they have that you would like to have? Which of those qualities do can you realistically develop? Create a plan for developing them.
- *Make a list of your strengths and weaknesses.* Continue to work on the weaknesses, of course, but be sure to use the new role as an opportunity to leverage your strengths, especially strengths you didn't get to use fully in your old role.
- *Get your story straight.* When you start at a new company, especially in a leadership role, you will have many opportunities to meet new people and tell them about yourself. Spend time refining your story about yourself and stick to it.

The story must be based on facts, of course, but it should deliver the story you want known about you. Write out a few paragraphs and then read them through your new co-workers' eyes. Is it a story that inspires confidence? Is it a story that positions you as an experienced leader? Is it a story that positions you as a likeable person? Your story should not be arrogant (don't make it a litany of all your grand accomplishments), but it shouldn't be overly humble and self-deprecating either—you need to come across as someone who is confident and competent, but not a self-absorbed jerk.

- *Be very clear about your values and expectations, and be sure everyone knows up front what you expect.* This issue is closely tied to "get your story straight." We are natural story-making creatures. When we encounter others, especially people in power, we try to figure them out and we do so by creating a narrative about them. We use the information we have for the narrative, but we tend to fill in the blanks with our own biases and assumptions. Leaders in new roles need to make sure they don't leave important blank spaces in the narrative—people should know what your values and expectations are so they don't make (and act upon) wrong assumptions.

- *Let people know how you like to be communicated to.* Some people like email, others hate it and prefer phone calls or face to face conversations. Nothing frustrates subordinates more than a leader who seems unresponsive. They create reasons for the lack of responsiveness that become part of the narrative, and they are usually not flattering. Much of this frustration occurs because no one figures out that they are simply using the wrong mechanism to communicate to each other. Therefore, let people know right away what is the best way to reach you and how you like to receive information.

- *Remember that everything you say or do sends a message, and act accordingly.* Most leaders have an internal narrative about themselves as just a "regular" person who should be treated as

58

"one of the team." When someone has been in a company for a long time, they actually were once "just" part of the team and probably struggled to balance that history with the executive distance needed in leadership roles. Subordinates need to see the leader as someone who stands above the team—an authority they can turn to when they need guidance, support, or reinforcement. Excessive humility will undermine the subordinates' confidence in a leader.

Subordinates are also aware that the leader's decisions can affect—positively or not—their future in the company. Accordingly, they observe and interpret everything the leader does and try to figure out any possible implications to their own self-interests. When leaders gets too comfortable they can forget the impact their words and deeds can have on the team—their humor and their frustrations send messages that are amplified beyond those of the average employee. Shrewd leaders use this to their advantage, showing extra-emotion at strategic times to send a deliberate message. Forgetting amplification and letting your guard down at the wrong time has the opposite effect, damaging your reputation more than you might realize.

While this blog is focused on leaders in transition, all leaders should remember these things and implement them—working on your personal leadership brand is something you should be doing all the time.

*There are a number of good books on planning for your first 100 days in a new role; I like "You're in Charge–Now What?" by Neff and Citrin.

Executive Presence–Slow Down

This may sound a little silly, but if you want to convey more executive presence, slow down and carry less.

I was recently talking with Dave, a director of engineering for a manufacturing company. He had just come from a meeting where he presented the product roadmap to a group of senior technology leaders for the company and was struck by how relaxed they all seemed despite challenging market dynamics.

"They were all there on time, but none of them seemed to have rushed to get there. They ended the meeting exactly on time, and as they walked out you could tell they were already focused on the next thing. Here's something else… None of them carried more than a tablet–they would all write things on their tablet or iPhone; one or two had a small black notebook."

In contrast, Dave had come rushing to meet me when I arrived in the lobby for our meeting, slightly frazzled and out of breath. He's a very tall man, and I had trouble keeping up with him as we walked from the lobby to his office. I noticed his brief case sitting in the corner–more a box on wheels, actually, that contained thick binders filled with reports, detailed procedures, and meeting notes. He told me that it is what he had taken to the product roadmap meeting.

While I wasn't in the meeting, my guess was that Dave looked like he was there to fix the TV rather than to confidently set the roadmap for the organization.

The term "executive presence" implies that one be "present," mentally being where you are rather than somewhere else. If we want people to think we have presence, we have to ensure that we are focused on what is in front of us, not what will be in front of us in the future or what was in front of us an hour ago. To use the old Sixties phrase, we have to "be here now." Someone who is always rushing around and dashing through the halls does not look present–they give the impression of being somewhere else in their mind while their body is trying to catch up. Someone who is carrying a lot looks unprepared, as if they are unsure what they might need so they brought everything. Confident leaders with executive presence walk deliberately and carry only what they absolutely have to so they are not distracted by clutter.

Take a look at the picture of Dwight Eisenhower that accompanies this article (you can find it at https://en.wikipedia.org/wiki/George_S._Patton). Here is the top Allied general during World War II talking with two other top generals. Do you think anyone ever had more pressure on their shoulders? Do you think anyone ever had more items on their to-do list? Yet, Ike seems calm, relaxed and solid. His hands are empty and he looks completely at ease. He looks present, and he certainly had executive presence.

So the next time you are tempted to dash off to your next meeting, be like Ike—slow down, be where you are, be at ease but in control.

Executive Presence: Communication

"Executive presence" is a broad and general term for the often-indefinable qualities we see in leaders. Everyone knows it when they see it, but they can't quite put their finger on why some people have it and why some don't. Executive presence is not the same as charisma; charisma helps but some people are not particularly charismatic and have strong executive presence, others have a lot of charisma but you wouldn't want them running your business.

When it is difficult to define something precisely, one ends up talking about particular qualities of the thing. That's how it is with executive presence, so this is the first in a series of blog posts on the topic and this one will focus on communication.

People with executive presence are good communicators. They are articulate, they have a relatively large vocabulary, they speak in complete sentences rather than fragments, and they are able to present their ideas in a narrative that makes sense–that is, it is coherent from point A to point B. Executive communication is not rushed, but it gets directly to the point.

This last issue, of getting directly to the point, is a common important developmental milestone for leaders who move from mid-level roles to senior roles, or for those who want to shine in front of the senior leadership team.

Take Will, for example. Will was the director of product management for a medium-sized business unit who was, by all accounts, brilliant and capable. He was articulate and well spoken, and could give very detailed overviews of market conditions, business opportunities, and what products under development would fit what customer need. Will was the go-to guy when the senior leaders in the organization wanted information about the market, but what he didn't realize was that they considered him to be too talkative. During his 360 assessment, someone said "He's the kind of guy who, if you ask him which pie is good in the cafeteria, gives you the history of pie before recommending the cherry or the apple."

Will is not alone in communicating this way—we often feel like we need to help others understand how we arrived at our conclusions so we start with the background and walk through all the variables, finally arriving at the main point. This works okay at lower levels, but it tends to irritate busy senior leaders.

There is a better way and the secrets to executive level communication are the same as the secrets to writing a good newspaper article: you say the most important thing first, followed by the second and third most important things, and then give the background if you have time or if the reader (or listener) is still interested.

Journalists are taught to write in a pyramid structure where the single most important sentence is written first, followed by other facts and details of descending importance. Journalists write this way because when you are reading the newspaper over your bowl of cornflakes in the morning you are probably only reading a sentence or two of each article and moving on to the next until you come across something that you are really interested in and decide to read deeper. Also, if an editor has to shorten an article due to space considerations, she does not want to have to read through the whole article and decide what to cut and what to keep, she just wants to cut off as much as she has to from the bottom.

Therefore, a news article doesn't start with the background ("It was a sunny day in Philadelphia…"); it gets to the point ("The Eagles defeated the Giants 36-21…"). Interested readers can read on for the details; others have found out what they wanted to know and can move on to something else.

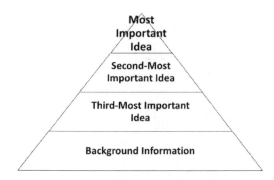

Anyone talking to senior leaders faces similar challenges—they have short attention spans and you never know how much time you will get before you are cut off. Therefore, you better learn to say the important things first and only provide as much background detail as they want you to. A good rule of thumb is that you should focus on, at most, three key ideas, and you should know what those three ideas are before you start talking. The pyramid model from Journalism 101 is a good way to think about how you should communicate to leaders—get right to the important main points, provide details as necessary.

Succinctness will give you the appearance of having more executive presence, but it is also important that you "put a bow" on your communications; that is, you must suggest a plan for resolving any issues raised. People with executive presence don't raise problems and leave them hanging unresolved in the room; they initiate solutions.

Yes, eloquence, articulateness, and the ability to tell a good story are all valuable qualities to have and useful in the appropriate context. But if you want to rise in an organization and if you want to be thought of as someone with executive presence, you have to master the art of executive communication and get right to the point, and then point to a solution.

Focus on Your Strengths? At Your Own Peril...

A decade ago, strengths-based management was all the rage. Managers were told not to try to "fix" or "change" people; instead, they should find out what that person's strengths are and put them in a role where they can use those strengths.

This approach works well at lower levels of an organization, but it can be career-ending for an executive to neglect identifying and working on weaknesses.

The higher one moves in an organization, the more impact one has on the success or failure of the organization, and weaknesses have more impact. Both strengths *and* weaknesses are amplified. I always tell my clients, "You get hired for your strengths, but you will get fired for your weaknesses."

This is not to say that everyone needs to be great at everything–that is simply not possible–and it is very good to understand your strengths and leverage them. We should avoid areas of responsibility in areas where we know we are weak or lack interest. If you are Michael Jordan, stick to basketball. Also, it is not necessary to fix *irrelevant* weaknesses. I can't hit a curveball, but it doesn't make sense to devote countless hours to developing that skill if I am not a baseball player.

However, leaders and executives need to focus on ruthlessly identifying and fixing relevant weaknesses–those areas which have an effect on one's current role or the role one wishes to have. Since our environment is always changing and marketplace demands continually shift, continual self-evaluation and adjustment is one of the main characteristics that separates the best from the high-potentials-who-never-were.

If you want to ensure that you will continue to grow in your career, or at least continue to succeed at the level you are at, here are some things you can do:

1. *Become disciplined about looking for ways to improve.* At the end of each week (or at whatever frequency seems best for you), do a simple after-action analysis. Ask these questions:

- What did I do well last week?

- What did I *not* do well?

- What could I do better next week?

Be unemotional about the analysis–it is not about blame or guilt–it is about gathering data and finding ways to improve.

2. *Get feedback.* Self-analysis is good, but it is very easy to fool yourself and, by definition, we can't see our blind spots. Solicit feedback from people you trust. Unfortunately, getting useful feedback can be difficult–not everyone is comfortable giving direct and candid feedback, especially to people in power. This is where a 360 assessment can be helpful–it is filtered through an objective and disinterested party and people are often more willing to give feedback through a filter. Call it a professional bias, but I think 360s via verbal interviews are generally more effective than online assessments. When I conduct an assessment interview I ask very simple and open-ended questions:

- What are this person's strengths? (To make sure those strengths are being used.)

- What do they need to be better at? (To identify two or three critical developmental areas. You want to make sure you getting feedback on relevant issues, whereas a standardized assessment can draw the focus to areas that may be weak but irrelevant because the seek to measure predetermined competencies.)

- What do you see as this person's future? What might stop them from getting there? (To get a sense of how much "runway" people think you have and to identify what competencies or skills you need to get to the next level.

3. *Get a coach or mentor.* We all need help. Even the best athletes have coaches; the best leaders in business and politics seek to learn from those who have been there before. We often don't see the obstacles we put in our own way, and there are things we won't be able to figure out on our own. A coach or mentor, whether from inside the organization or outside, is invaluable.

Power: How to Get it and Why

"Power tends to corrupt, and absolute power corrupts absolutely."

(Lord Acton)

Acton may be correct (most people leave out the important word "tends" when repeating this quote), but I have never seen an effective leader who was power*less*. In fact, the best leaders are powerful people who know how to use power appropriately.

Most of us can find many examples that validate Lord Acton's concern—from the tyrannical political ruler to the bossy new manager who lets a little power go his or her head. This can lead to us being wary of people who seem to seek power and to avoid talking about the importance of power in organizations.

However, leaders who don't come to terms with the realities of power and it's appropriate and ethical use eventually become ineffectual victims of circumstance or, in the other extreme, examples of Acton's dictum. In simple terms, the best leaders accumulate power and use effectively and ethically; the worst accumulate it and use it poorly or don't know how to accumulate it and fail because of impotence.

The first step in coming to terms with power and its use is to recognize that power is value-neutral. Power, at it's most basic, is simply the capacity to produce a result; it is up to the individual to determine what kind of result it is used to produce. Used effectively, power can build a kingdom; used ineffectively or inappropriately it can destroy a nation.

The second step is to understand the nature of power. My favorite writer and theorist on power in organizations was David McClelland, who taught at Harvard University for 30 years beginning in 1956. In 1976, he co-authored (with David Burnham) an influential article for the *Harvard Business Review* called "Power is the Great Motivator." From McClelland's perspective, power is a natural part of the human experience, and what matters most is whether it is used in a mature way for the good of the group or it is used in an immature way for the benefit of the individual at the expense of the group.

Power Motivation

McClelland is primarily remembered for his motivation theory, which states that leaders are motivated by three primary needs: affiliation (nAff), achievement (nAch), and power (nPow). Everyone has all three needs, but they are present in varying proportions in each person. McClelland and Burnham conducted a study of leaders and found some intriguing correlations between leadership effectiveness and motivation. In short, they concluded that those leaders with a high need for affiliation tended to be least effective, and those with a high need for power tended to be the most effective—as long as they also had a high degree of personal inhibition. Those with a very high need for achievement actually struggled as leaders for a very specific set of reasons.

The need for affiliation is, at its core, a need to be liked by others. A person with a high need for affiliation desires harmonious relationships with other people and they need to feel accepted. They tend to conform to the norms of their work group and prefer work that provides significant personal interaction. While the ability to get along with others and connect at an emotional level are important in most leadership situations, the study showed that high nAff leaders often failed because they tried to make too many people happy and struggled to make difficult business decisions. They often fail to give constructive feedback to their employees and tell their employees only what they think the employee will want to hear. They also have a tendency to make *ad hoc* and *ad hominem* decisions. This style creates a lack of consistency and clarity regarding policies and procedures, ultimately making subordinates feel like they have little responsibility for outcomes. Motivation and pride in their work tends to be lowest in employees led by high nAff leaders.

The need for achievement relates to the desire to accomplish and exceed goals. People with a high achievement need seek to excel and want to do things better than they have been done before. They tend to thrive in entrepreneurial situations and prefer to work alone or with other high-achievers. Surprisingly, high nAch leaders tend to struggle when they get to high levels of the organization because they tend to be*doers* rather than effective *delegators*. They struggle in situations where they are removed from hands-on activities and are required to spend more and more of their time managing others. High nAch leaders need frequent feedback and a short-term rewards system so they can continually measure their progress. They quickly become frustrated with bureaucracies and often end up frustrated when they don't feel like they can immediately get involved in direct problem solving.

Those with a high power need are focused on shaping their environment and influencing others rather than the satisfaction of immediate feedback. McClelland and Burnham found that the most effective leaders tended to be those who had a need for power that was higher than their need to be liked and their need for achievement.

However, even people with a high power need could be separated into two categories:

- Personal power (pPow) leaders, who have a desire to direct others, and

- Institutional or social leaders (sPow), who have a desire to organize the efforts of others to advance the goals of the organization or group.

The key differentiator between these two groups was the degree of self-control or "inhibition" displayed by the leader; institutional leaders had high power drive mixed with high inhibition while personal power (pPow) leaders tended to combine high power drive with low inhibition.

Approaches to Power

According to McClelland and Burnham, while personal power leaders were more effective than high nAff or nAch leaders, they tended to put their own needs before the needs of the organization. They can be charismatic and inspirational, but the inspiration tends to be centered on a select group of loyal followers. They lack the discipline to be institution builders, focused on short-term victories and when the pPow leader leaves, the team left behind is often disorganized and morale quickly erodes. Further, pPow leaders often demonstrated problematic behaviors including rudeness, alcohol and substance abuse, sexual exploitation of subordinates, and fondness for the symbols of prestige such as expensive cars and large offices.

By contrast, institutional leaders—those with high nPow and high inhibition—are less egotistic and less defensive; their self-image is not directly connected to their job; they seek advice from experts; and they take a long-range view. According to McClelland and Burnham's study they were the most effective at instilling a sense of responsibility, creating organizational clarity, and building team spirit. They attributed these qualities to the sPow leader's self-control, which allowed them to direct their power toward the benefit of the institution as a whole rather than being put to use for the leader's personal aggrandizement.

Further, sPow leaders had the following qualities:

- They are organization-minded—they like to join groups and they feel responsible for building them.

- They believe in the importance of centralized authority.

- They like to work and have a high need to get things done in orderly way.

- They are willing to sacrifice self-interest for benefit of the organization.

- They have a keen sense of justice, believing that all who work hard should and will be rewarded.

- They emphasize building loyalty to the organization and creating sense of lasting team cohesion and organizational clarity.

- They empower people in an effort to make subordinates feel strong rather than weak.

- They help people get things done rather than focusing on their personal needs.

A critical differentiator between sPow and pPow leaders, according to McClelland, is maturity, which "involves the ability to use whatever mode is appropriate to the situation. Immaturity involves using perhaps only one mode in all situations or using a mode inappropriate to a particular situation."

Stages of Power

McClelland identified four stages of power orientation. The stages are based on a simple matrix comprising two dimensions:

- Whether the source of power is inside ("*I* have the power") or outside ("*It* has the power"), and

- Whether the object of the power is the self or something else.

There are adaptive and maladaptive versions of all four stages, and while the stages roughly correlate to stages of ego-development models of Freud, Erikson, and others, the stages are also concurrent through life and it is possible to demonstrate adaptive behaviors in a higher stage and maladaptive behaviors in a lower stage.

Each stage can be summarized by a simple internal message.

In Stage I, the message is *"'It' strengthens me."* For the child at this stage, the source of the power is outside of the individual—the parent, the institution, the deity, etc.—and the object that is being acted on is the individual themselves. Adults in this stage align themselves with powerful others and tend to thrive in situations where they can serve powerful people—the boss, the political leader, an assertive spouse. Taken to an extreme, people in Stage I can be totally dependent on a powerful individual, substances, a social group, or their religion.

In Stage II, the message is *"I strengthen myself."* The source of power is the individual and someone in this stage uses it to act on themselves. The child begins to develop a sense of control and realization that they need not rely on others for their sense of power. They start to exert control of objects and become identified with their possessions; toys become symbols of power (a pattern that extends into adulthood for many Stage II-focused individuals, who accumulate symbols of prestige). This is also the world of self-help and self-actualization, and taken to an extreme it can result in obsessive-compulsive behavior.

In Stage III, the message is *"I have impact on others."* Again, the source of power is the individual, but now it is used to act on the other. The young person begins to learn to feel powerful by controlling others, learning to manipulate and desiring to compete. People "who fixate in this modality...always try to outwit, outmaneuver, and defeat other people—in sports, in work, in arguments, and even in ordinary social relationships." Oddly enough, displays of altruistic-seeming behavior can be seen in people at Stage III, as the individual gives as a way of (consciously or not) controlling the relationship, establishing a position of superiority by being the one who can help the other. At the extreme, Stage III power becomes smothering, dominating, and abusive.

At Stage IV, the message is *"'It' moves me to do my duty."* The source of power is outside—the institution, the organization, the group, or the cause—and it is used by the individual to act in service of others. "Great religious and political leaders from Jesus Christ to Abraham Lincoln and Malcolm X have felt they were instruments of a higher power which is beyond self. Their goal was to act on others on behalf of this higher authority," according to McClelland. At a more mundane level, the institutional leader described earlier is functioning at Stage IV. Taken to the extreme, however, Stage IV power leads to messianism, and the individual can commit acts of violence in the name of the higher power to which he or she is identified.

How to Become More Powerful

Once we get over our discomfort with the idea of power and understand the stages of power, it becomes easier to acquire and use. Here are some tips:

1. *Recognize that knowledge truly is power.* Competence and skill in your field, basic leadership/management skills, and an understanding of human nature are the entry-level requirements for being powerful. Work constantly to improve in these areas or nothing else will help.

2. *Understand the power of relationships.* It is part of human nature that we do things for people who do things for us. Others are more willing to help us achieve our goals if we have helped them in the past; especially if we have done so, ironically, without the expectation of reciprocation. The most powerful people are the ones who empower others reflexively rather than with an eye to personal gain.

3. *Observe and analyze the most powerful people around you.* Do a best-practice analysis of powerful people you interact with or observe.

What do they seem to have in common? Which of those behaviors can you develop?

4. *Study the principles of power.* The scope of this article does not allow for a list of tactical behaviors related to power, but I'll recommend some good sources to learn more:

- *Biographies of powerful people.* I'm not a big fan of business-leader biographies that try to boil leadership down to a few easy principles–especially those written by former CEOs, which tend to be a self-glorifying and not always focused on what actually made the person successful. But there is value in reading historical biographies of powerful people, such as Churchill, Lincoln, Washington, Ataturk, and the recently deceased Lee Kuan Yew; they tend to get us into the mindset of the subject and often provide more accurate and less self-serving tactical advice on power dynamics.

- *Books on power.* David McClelland's "Power: The Inner Experience" is both difficult to find and a bit dense at times, but it explores the psychology of power better than any book I've seen. I like Jeffrey Pfeffer's "Power: Why Some people Have It—and Others Don't" a good book on the basics of power in organizations. "Warfighting: The US Marine Corps Book of Strategy" is an indispensable little primer that applies to business as well as battle. I'm also a fan of Wharton's Charles E. Dwyer's book "The Shifting Sources of Power and Influence." Finally, though it is almost a cliche to recommend it, Sun Tzu's "The Art of War" is a valuable resource.

While we might be uncomfortable with the idea of power, you simply can't get anything done without it. If you are a leader who does not learn how to acquire and use power, you will be ineffective. The best way to make sure you don't fulfill Acton's dictum is go be a student of power and master the art of using it ethically.

Instinctual Leadership: Signaling Warmth and Competence

Humans are contradictory creatures. We have the capacity to step back, think rationally, and reason through complex problems, but we often don't use that capacity—relying instead on snap judgments to guide us.

Daniel Kahneman's book, "Thinking, Fast and Slow," popularized the idea that we have two "systems" for thinking:

- System 1 is "fast" thinking, which relies on emotion, naïve intuition, and non-conscious mental models or "rules of thumb" (called "heuristics") that are part of our evolutionary heritage. System 1 is very useful in helping us quickly solve simple problems and respond to threats (*a rustle in the bushes=predator=run!*), but not so good on more-complicated matters that require careful assessment.

- System 2 is "slow" thinking, which makes use of our ability to pause, evaluate, consider options, test hypotheses, etc. System 2 is more accurate, but not as fast and it requires more energy. Thus, we have evolved to use it less, saving energy and erring on the side of seeing predators in the bushes or other threats even when they are not there—better safe than sorry, after all…

Both of these systems are valuable and have their drawbacks if used in the wrong context. Fast thinking helps us solve simple problems quickly but can lead to simplistic responses to complex problems; slow thinking helps us solve complex problems accurately but can be paralyzing if we keep seeking more data than the problem requires. The trick–and it's a difficult trick–is to know when to use which system of thinking.

This dual-system processing profoundly affects our response to leaders. Most of the books about "conscious," "enlightened," "servant," etc. leadership are appealing to System 2—yes, when we stop to think about it, we would like these kinds of leaders. But working under the surface is System 2, which responds to a very different set of stimuli—and it responds in a more primal or instinctual way. Thus, leaders face a dilemma—our "slow thinking" pushes us to say we want one thing but we tend to respond in ways that contradict what we say when our instinctual needs are heightened.

The best leaders understand this and develop a set of skills and competencies that satisfy both systems. They have the ability to sense and respond to what system is needed, an ability I call "Instinctual Leadership."

Instinctual Leadership includes a variety of skills that fall into a few broad categories, including:

• Mastery of the requisite management and execution skills (by "requisite" I mean those necessary for the particular situation).

• Self-awareness and emotional intelligence based on a requisite understanding of human nature (see "A Leader's Guide to How People Think" in this collection). (Leaders don't need to be professional psychologists, but it helps to know the basics—you can't win hearts and minds if you don't understand hearts and minds.)

• Excellent critical thinking skills that help us avoid the potential errors of emotion-based, System 1 thinking.

• An understanding of the three instinctual biases—preserving, navigating, and transmitting—that influence what aspects of business and leadership we focus on and which we ignore, often to our detriment.

In this article, I want to focus on a very specific instinctual dynamic that shapes how we respond to leadership: the need to see both warmth and competence in our leaders.

It helps to see it in terms of evolutionary advantage in social species in order to understand this dynamic. In almost any social species, a group will have an "alpha" male and/or female. The alpha is dominant—getting its needs met first but also being looked to for guidance or protection in times of danger. The alpha eats first, but the rest of the group will look to it for signals of how to respond to threats—if the alpha fights back they will all fight back; if the alpha flees they will all flee. If the alpha makes poor decisions, or proves to be untrustworthy or dangerous by taking too much advantage of its privileged position, the followers will rebel and overthrow the alpha.

Human dynamics may be more complex than other social species, but the fundamentals are the same—we look for leaders who are competent and strong, but also "trustworthy enough." By "trustworthy enough," I mean that followers have to believe that while the leader may be flawed, he or she will not betray "us," however "us" is defined.

One of the ways we humans signal trustworthiness is through displays of "warmth," the leader's ability to show enough empathy and approachability that the individuals in the group believe the leader will treat them fairly. Someone with warmth will consider "our" needs and not stab us in the back; someone who is competent will be able to meet the challenges of leadership that arise from both within and from outside of the group. Thus, at an instinctual level we look for warmth and competence in our leaders.

Aloof or "cold" leaders, even if they highly competent, will lose the support of followers—an aloof leader may make a mercenary decision that doesn't protect the needs of those in the tribe. Followers, feeling unprotected, will not rally emotionally around a leader from whom they feel no warmth.

Likewise, empathic or "warm" leaders will lose the support of followers if they are not competent enough. If the leader cannot deliver results, the whole team fails; people are fired, bonuses are not paid, market share is lost.

Sustainable leadership involves developing both warmth and competence and being able to signal to others that one has those qualities.

"Signal" is the critical word here. In biology, signals are behaviors or qualities that send a message that lead others to believe something particular about an individual. A classic example is the peacock's feathers, which send a message to the pea-hen that the peacock is healthy and robust, making him a suitable mate. In reality, not every peacock with spectacular feathers is a suitable mate, but the probability is higher that they are and pea-hens have evolved an attraction to them. Evolution is a wise gambler and always plays the odds.

Leaders, like all of us, send signals whether they are aware of them or not. Team members infer, consciously or not, messages from the behaviors and qualities of the leader. The aggregate of these messages shape how the leader is perceived and ultimately influence how effective and sustainable the leader will be; the right signals inspire trust and followership, the wrong signals erode them.*

Note that that we are talking about messages and impressions when we talk about signals, not facts. Someone may seem warm but may not actually be empathic or trustworthy, which is how con artists operate. Someone may seem far more competent than they actually are and get into a role that is beyond their abilities. A discerning leader is able to see beyond the signals and look for the substance, they understand that their System 1 picks will tell a compelling intuitive narrative but that in important matters it must it must also pass the System 2 test of careful evaluation.

That some signals are misrepresentative, however, is not a reason to ignore the importance and power of the signals we send. Because someone else appears warm but is actually a jerk is not reason for you to be aloof; that someone else falsely signals competence is not a good enough reason for you to resist signaling *your* competence.

Another important point to note is that while you can never be too competent, it *is* possible to be too warm. Beyond a certain point there seems to be diminishing returns on additional warmth. People need to think the leader is warm, but not soft. The leader has to be able to be forceful and, to a degree, even intimidating when circumstances require it. Too much forcefulness, however, sends a message of a lack of empathy that has much the same effect as "coldness" and erodes trust.

The lesson from this is that leaders need to continually develop competence while cultivating enough warmth to build trust among those they lead. They need to demonstrate those qualities, not by pretending to be something they are not, but by being attuned to and demonstrating the behaviors or qualities that signal warmth and competence.

––––––––

*In my role as executive coach I am often asked to help people develop their "executive presence," but rarely can anyone define what they mean by the term. I believe that what they are trying to capture is the combination of warmth, competence, and effective signaling that is felt implicitly but difficult to describe explicitly.

The Empty Cup

Some people already know everything, and are more than happy to let you know it, even when they claim to be asking your opinion.

In the Zen Buddhist tradition, there is the parable of the tea cup that can help us from being one of those people.

A scholar from the west knocks on the door of a venerable zen master and announces, "I would like to learn from you."

The zen master invites him in and the scholar proceeds to tell the master everything he knows about zen. The master waits for his visitor to stop, but he just keeps going. In time, the master starts to prepare tea. He boils the water, puts the tea in the pot and waits for it to steep; he prepares the cups. All the while, the scholar talks.

The zen master begins to pour tea for his guest, slowly and carefully. When the tea reaches the brim, the master continues pouring and the tea runs down the side of the cup and across the table. The scholar leaps back to avoid the hot tea and says, "Stop! It's already full."

The zen master stops pouring, looks at the scholar and quietly says, "Your mind is like this cup; it is already full. You must first empty your cup if you want to taste my tea."

The lesson here is that if we want to learn we must stop talking and listen. We must understand that others have much to teach us if we allow them to do so. We need to remind ourselves that it is okay to say, "I don't know."

We must do our best to not be full-cuppers.

Being Mindful

Flipping through a recent issue of a prominent business magazine, I came across yet another article on how organizations are flocking to "mindfulness" training based on traditional Eastern practices. In fact, according to the article some 22% of companies offer such mindfulness training for their employees.

There is a lot to be said for such practices, but there is more than one way to become mindful and I prefer the kind of mindfulness work that focuses on developing relaxed, deliberate, and purposeful thought rather than simply breathing and observing our thoughts and inner states.

The psychologist Ellen Langer has written about how to develop this kind of mindfulness in her book, "Mindfulness." Langer's version of mindfulness has three fundamental qualities:

- Creation of new categories (seeing beyond the traditional habitual and limited understanding of a situation),

- Openness to new information, and

- Awareness of more than one perspective.

In this article, I'd like to talk about how we can better develop this kind of mindset. Because of the specific connotations that many have of "mindfulness" as a specific traditional eastern practice, I prefer to talk about "awareness," which is perception of a situation or fact. For me, "awareness" involves actually seeing what is in front of us, reducing illusion, and accurately assessing our environment. It has the dual qualities of presence and thoughtfulness.

In order to develop this kind of awareness, we need three skills:

- *Being present*–training ourselves to manage our attention and direct it where we need to direct it.

- *Noticing*–skills for seeing what is happening to us and in front of us, especially things that we might otherwise overlook.

- *Processing*–skillful contemplation and (when necessary) action based on what we notice.

Practices for Becoming Present:

It happens to us all the time—someone starts talking to us and before we know it we are thinking about lunch, the meeting after lunch, the ride home at the end of the day and the pothole that we hit this morning and that the tires need to be rotate, and, oh, I have to get the kids to baseball practice tonight but first pick up milk and… oh, wait, he's still talking, I better listen…

Being present means the ability to set all those things aside and pay attention to what is happening now; awareness training involves extending the length of time we are able to do that.

A first step in being present can be quite simple: Tell yourself "Take a deep breath." After you take the breath and exhale it, tell yourself, "OK, be here and pay attention." Every time you find that you have drifted off, repeat the process. The key is to practice it; you'll be amazed at the results.

If you want to really work on this skill, there is great value in learning how do perform a centering breath, a practice similar to what is typically thought of as Eastern-based mindfulness training and is very useful for relaxation and stress reduction. Many good books and websites provide information for this.

I've never really had the patience for seated meditation exercises but I have found that deliberate physical activities to be very useful in helping one focus on the present. For me, martial-arts training was great for this. There is nothing like the prospect of being punched in the nose or hit with a bamboo sword sheathed in deer-skin leather to teach you to "be here now." (There was a very good reason for the samurai to adopt the practice of zen.) However, there are many less-vivid ways to get this experience.

Practices for Noticing:

We can't be "present" all the time. Some people strive for this, and some people claim to have achieved it, but I see nothing wrong with simply zoning out on occasion and letting the mind monkeys jump from branch to branch. The problem we must guard against is failing to pay attention when we need to pay attention.

The first application of "noticing," therefore, is to notice signals from our bodies or our environment that we need to be present. Our emotions are the non-conscious mind's way of signaling to us that we need to pay attention to something. Do you feel anger? Sorrow? Shame? These are signals that there is something happening around you or to you and that you need to pay attention and take corrective action.

A simple exercise is to practice monitoring our emotions. When we notice an emotional state we should practice naming it and exploring what it is pointing to. We can ask: What am I feeling? Why am I feeling this way? Is there a situation that needs to be resolved? How can I resolve it?

The objective of this simple activity is to, over time, reduce the amount of time that passes between when we feel an emotion and to recognize that we are feeling it. Often, we can walk around for hours being angry, obsessing over what someone did to us or over something we failed to do, but never truly realizing we are angry. Eventually, we may resolve the situation that made us angry, or we may not resolve it but the anger may dissipate on its own. But we have lost a lot of time and energy in the interim. By working to reduce the time between when we experience an emotion and when we recognize it and take corrective action, we reduce that loss. With time and practice we get better at recognizing our emotions as they arise and managing them in real time, allowing us to avoid the damage we do to ourselves and others while in the grips of the negative emotions.

Noticing also involves truly seeing and considering our surroundings. The brain has a tendency to minimize what we perceive–most of what is happening around us is lost to our awareness. This is an evolved pattern that allows us to, primarily, focus on threats to our well-being– if a predator is chasing us, the beautiful sunset is not very important. Likewise, blurring out most of our environment allowed our ancestors' brains to reserve fuel and apply itself to more practical issues. Tunnel vision and mindlessness were adaptive qualities that helped our ancestors survive long enough to pass those qualities on to us.

We live in different times than our ancestors, however, and today we have the luxury of being more mindful and experience more than just the minimum necessary for survival. Such deeper noticing provides both a richer inner life and more effective interactions with our environment—noticing adds both enjoyment and efficacy to our lives.

There are many exercises for learning to practice noticing. The idea behind all of them is to train ourselves to see things we might not ordinarily see. Here are a few:

The 'Trane Technique:

The sublime jazz musician John Coltrane recommended listening to a song this way: First, listen to the whole song without paying particular attention to anything; just let it wash over you. Second, listen to it for one instrument at a time. Play the song and focus on the saxophone. Play it again and listen to the drums. Play it again and listen to the piano, etc. Finally, play it again and just let it wash over and pay attention to how it affects you physically and emotionally. You'll be surprised by what you find out.

Reacquaint with the Everyday:

It is easy to take for granted our everyday environments and the people we encounter therein. For this practice, go to a place you go every day, whether it be your own kitchen or the local coffee shop. Take a moment to truly notice the place. Look at the individual items in it. Pay attention to the texture and shapes. Notice the smells. Listen to the sounds. Consciously identify something you never paid attention to before. At the coffee shop, notice the barista: What color are his eyes? Is he wearing a name badge? If so, what is his name? Does he seem happy in what he does? What kind of shoes is he wearing? Are his laces tied? Does he have any visible tattoos? The questions are endless.

Do not judge the barista! The objective is to *notice without judgment*. It is only by training ourselves to notice without judgment that we can be truly open to new information as Langer suggests rather than starting the comfortable slide into habitual judgments and mindlessness. When we judge we see what we expect to see rather than what is.

Observe cues and clues:

My wife would be the first to say that I can be oblivious to some of the everyday things that happen around me, and I agree. I can go a very long time without noticing a new piece of furniture, that the furniture has been moved, etc. Most of us, to our detriment, take our home environment as an "attention-free" zone where we take things for granted until something becomes an inconvenience. Noticing can bring our most mundane experiences alive again.

Despite my frequent obliviousness at home, I think that the most important skill a coach like me can have is the ability to notice, and I find my clients' offices to be an important place to practice these skills.

What pictures hang on the wall or are framed on the desk? Are they placed where the client can see them or where visitors can see them? What memorabilia is on their shelves? What kind of cell phone do they carry? Where do they keep it when they are not using it? What kinds of words do they use–big words, small words, jargon? Do they speak fast or slow? Do they seem rooted in their body or uncomfortable? Do they look tired or well-rested; distracted or focused? All of these things are cues and clues, not to necessarily make an assessment of the person, but to help identify what kind of questions to ask to find out what is really important for me to know. Again, examples of things we can notice are almost countless and bounded only by the limits of your curiosity, but if the pictures face the visitor it would be interesting to know if it signals particular pride in the family or is it just happenstance? We can ask, "What a nice-looking family, can you tell me about them?" to better understand the client's personal values. A professional award tucked on a bookcase is an opportunity to ask about what the client values as career accomplishments. Recently, I saw a boxing glove peeking out of a gym bag on the client's office floor; my asking about it led to a conversation first about health and mixed-martial arts and eventually to a conversation about aging and finding comfort in your own place in life as you reach your mid-40s (and beyond, in my case…). I learned far more about my client in that conversation than I did from reading his impressive CV.

Anyone can use these same techniques as a way of practicing noticing, and the things one learns from noticing can be invaluable for leaders.

The key is not to judge the other person, but to notice–to be open, receptive, and curious–so you can find out what is really important to them and what they really need. This is the root of true compassion–experiencing people as they are rather than as we expect them to be or want them to be. We only truly understand people when we truly see them, and we only truly see them when we take the time to notice.

Practices for Processing:

While we shouldn't judge what we notice, we do need to learn to analyze it; judgment implies assessing subjective value but analysis implies methodical examination so we can better understand something. It is crucial to develop tools for analyzing those things we notice, the stories others tell us, or the stories we tell ourselves. Without tools for critical thinking–skepticism, an understanding of cognitive biases, skilled use of logic and the ability to identify logical fallacies, education in how to tell good information from bad–all the noticing and attention in the world will be of limited value. It is these skills that equip us to cut through our own nonsense, to challenge our internal narratives, to hold ourselves to a standard of integrity. They are crucial in effectively working with others for the same reasons; we can't help our clients or our coworkers or our customers if we let them hoodwink us.

Tools for developing those skills are abundant, and I will list some at the end of this article. That said, I have found that the most important qualities to have are a skeptical attitude–expecting the evidence to match a person's claim–and the willingness to relentlessly ask yourself two questions every time you recognize yourself stating an opinion: *How do I know I know that to be true?* and *Is there any evidence that points to me being wrong?* No one likes to be wrong, but everyone wants to learn new things; the truly mindful person understands that each time we realize we were wrong about something we have learned something new.

Emotional Intelligence–Without the Touchy-Feely Stuff

Emotional intelligence is, essentially, the ability to recognize and manage emotional states. While it is not quite the rage that it was 10 years ago, emotional intelligence is still an important quality for leaders to possess. That said, just the mere mention of "emotion"–especially "negative" emotions such as fear, shame, and sorrow–makes many people in organizations uncomfortable. Emotions cloud our judgment and make us vulnerable, right? Who wants that? We should just get back to work…

Not so fast.

What we often think of as negative emotions are actually useful early warning signals of problems in our environment. The emotional components of our brain pick up signals from our environment far more quickly and effectively than does the more conscious, deliberative part of our brain. (The popularity of emoticons is because they help to send emotional signals that register in our non-conscious but are not otherwise available in written communication.)

Emotions are often one part of our brain's attempt to tell another part of our brain to pay attention to something that could be important. Learning to recognize and heed those signals is a useful skill. For example, we should understand that:

•   Anger often indicates that we perceive that an injustice or inequity has been done to us and needs to be addressed.

•   Shame indicates we feel we have done something wrong and we need to correct it.

•   Fear indicates that we perceive a threat that we need to mitigate.

The emotional structures of our brain developed during a time when the behavioral options of "fight, flee, or comply" were sufficient to deal with the rigors of day-to-day life. Our environment is much more complicated today, however, and we need to learn to take better advantage of those emotional stimuli. With a little practice we can learn to value our emotions and use them as tools for problem solving.

Here is how to do that:

- *Learn to identify and name your emotions.* Ever feel angry for a while without really realizing it or knowing why? It happens frequently to most of us, and when someone asks us what we are angry about it may take a moment to figure out the root cause. Practice recognizing your emotional states as quickly as possible; eventually you will learn to see the emotions as they arise and you'll be hijacked by them less frequently.

- *Identify the cause of the emotion.* If you recognize that you are feeling anxiety, for example, ask yourself, "What, specifically, is causing me to feel this way?" Are you concerned about an upcoming sales call or worried that you didn't leave enough time to complete a project? Clearly identifying a problem is the first step to correcting the problem.

- *Let go of the emotion and begin working to solve the problem.* Carrying on a negative emotional state after we've identified the problem causing is like carrying the boat after we've crossed the river–it only makes the journey more cumbersome. Take a deep breath and as you exhale consciously release the emotions–feel the chemicals leaving your body. It's okay to experience emotions, it's not okay to allow ourselves to dwell in them after they have served their purpose. Once you let go of the emotion you can think rationally, develop a clear plan, and take appropriate action.

- *Leverage positive emotions–happiness, excitement, etc., to add energy to your activities.*

Good leaders don't fear emotions–either in themselves or in others. They see them as a useful evolutionary legacy and they learn how to manage them rather than being ruled by them. They also learn to recognize the emotional states of others so they can be more effective at helping others solve problems and motivating them.

How does that make you feel? Excited, I hope.

It Takes Toughness to Be a Truly Compassionate Leader

Watching a video* of a TED talk by Zen Buddhist teacher Joan Halifax made me think of the Enneagram-based leadership model I use with my executive clients. One of the components of the model is what I call "Leadership Relationships" and focuses on points 8, 5, and 2 of the Enneagram diagram. The premise is that in order to be a successful leader they must develop and skillfully use *power*, practice executive *detachment*, and be able to emotionally *connect* to people. Without power, leaders are ineffectual and will not be respected; without emotional connection they fail to win the hearts of employees and they will not be followed; without executive detachment they cannot make the difficult decisions leaders have to make.

These qualities are very similar to the qualities that Halifax identifies as being needed for true compassion, and her view reinforces for me the idea that learning to be a skillful leader is in many ways simply learning how to be a more skillful person.

Thus, the model I use for my executive clients can also be useful for anyone seeking more skillful relationships and an increased ability to be compassionate (something we can *all* use).

It's easy to see that the ability to emotionally connect with others is at the heart of compassion, but for many it stops there–they don't see why power and detachment are also necessary. In fact, on the surface power and detachment might seem to undermine compassion. Doesn't power imply control over others? Doesn't detachment imply a lack of compassion?

Not necessarily.

Power has many definitions and people bring a lot of baggage to the word. As Lord Acton famously said, "Power corrupts. Absolute power corrupts absolutely." Even in hard-charging business environments, people are conflicted when I start talking to them about the importance of the healthy acquisition and use of power. But if we are unable to look beyond these negative connotations we push our issues regarding power into the shadow, and from there they can cause a lot of trouble.

To overcome our discomfort with power we have to first understand what power actually is. According to Merriam-Webster online, *power* is the "ability to act or produce an effect." One of the requirements of having the ability to act is having strength, the ability to meet or endure the rigors of a task. This is the rationale behind the quote at the beginning of this article—we need a strong back to have a soft front, otherwise the soft front simply folds under a little pressure.

Here's an illustration of why we need strength:

The first time I ever witnessed extreme poverty was when I went to Istanbul some years ago. Don't get me wrong, I lived most of my adult life in the city and have, like most people, sadly encountered almost innumerable homeless people, and I have been in very poor neighborhoods in many US cities. But in the US we have more safety nets than a lot of places (though not enough from my perspective) and we don't see the kind of poverty here that exists in other places.

But Istanbul was different. Though a beautiful city with a lot of wealth, there was also more poverty than I had encountered before. I recall riding with my host—who was fairly wealthy—and stopping at a street light where the car was swarmed by children begging for coins. Thinking of my sons at home while I looked at these beautiful children, it broke my heart to try to imagine the kind of lives they lived. It was easier to look away.

I talked to my host, the father of young girls himself, afterward about the situation and found out that his strategy was similar.

"How do you deal with seeing that every day?" I asked.

"You shut it out of your mind," he said. "Otherwise it becomes too painful."

Stopping our own sympathy pains is one of the reasons we look away and stifle our ability to be compassionate—truly feeling the pain of other people is painful to us. We can only sustain it for so long before we become overwhelmed. If we are not strong, our compassion can quickly break us.

Power allows us to sustain compassion and to take compassionate action to help relieve the suffering of others. Power allows us to lift people up, if only by sometimes being a vessel for sharing their pain. I struggle to see how powerless and weak people are capable of true compassion, but we must also understand how to calibrate our power when we apply it. Sometimes people need comforting, other times they need a push; we must know when to do which, and when we push we need to know how hard to do so.

(This is the significance of the vertical arrow in the diagram—it represents the need to apply the correct amount of power for the situation.)

Leadership Relationships

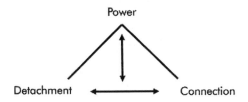

95

****

As Halifax also mentions in the video, we have to have a degree of *detachment* (or "non-attachment") to be truly compassionate. In fact, without the ability to detach from, observe, and manage our emotions we fall into the trap of what the Tibetan Buddhist teacher Chogyam Trungpa Rinpoche called *idiot's compassion*. Idiot's compassion can take multiple forms, including:

- Actions that stem from our own dysfunctional need to help others, whether or not they need or want our help. An example of this would be the "healer" who is subconsciously trying to treat themselves by projecting their own issues onto the client they think they are helping.

- Actions that come from a genuine sympathy for the situation of the other person but may actually make matters worse. Sometimes we just want to make someone's pain go away and don't think about the consequences of how we do it. The overly sensitive parent who jumps to satisfy a child's every desire is a fool indeed, and often ends up raising a brat.

Without the ability to detach–to step back and evaluate our reactions, to put the other person's needs and experience into context, to think about long-term implications of the actions we take out of sympathy–our compassion can do more damage than good. Compassion starts in the heart, but it should be guided by the head and supported by a strong belly.

Detachment can also help us extend our compassion by allowing us respite from the pain compassion can bring. Mindfulness and non-attachment serve to let us know when we need a break, when our power sources are depleted so we can protect ourselves by stepping back and recharging. It reminds us that compassion is a marathon and not a sprint, and keeps us from burning out too quickly. In practicing true compassion, emotional detachment must exist in a dynamic tension with our ability to emotionally connect. Too much of one is just as much a problem as too much of the other; we need them both at the same time.

(This dynamic tension is represented by the horizontal arrow in the diagram.)

****

As Halifax's TED talk reminds us, compassion is not a quality that resides fully in the heart–it requires a strong will and a clear mind, a lesson that also lies embedded in the Enneagram.

*https://www.ted.com/talks/joan_halifax?language=en#t-773943

Getting Smarter: Why Leaders, and the Rest of Us, Need to Be Better Thinkers

"Common sense is nothing more than a deposit of prejudices laid down by the mind before you reach eighteen." (Attributed to Albert Einstein in "Mathematics, Queen and Servant of the Sciences" (1952) by Eric Temple Bell)

We live in a time when we carry with us nearly all the information in the world (accurate and inaccurate) in the little computers in our pockets. Opinionators blare at us nonstop from cable news channels or flood our inboxes or Facebook streams with all manner of provocative claims. Marketers and politicians of all stripes serve up a steady stream of sound bites designed to activate our emotional triggers and they bombard us with dubious claims.

There are forms of intellectual quality control that attempt to protect us from the unending flow of bunk, but they are overwhelmed and inadequate. The small amount of objective public journalism still in existence, the shrinking number of leaders who seek truth rather than reelection or personal gain, and an educational system bowing to the pressure to prepare students for careers rather than citizenship just can't keep up with all the forces that could mislead us.

We live in a time when the demands on our ability to think about and evaluate our world outstrip the innate tools to do so—our "common sense"—and we need to supplement those tools with skills that are relatively easy to acquire with a little focus and discipline. How we can do that is the focus of this series and the "Critical Thinking for Leaders" training program that it is based on.

While the series and program are focused on leadership, all of the skills we are talking about are applicable to life in general—how we relate to each other; how we make decisions about our finances, our health, our careers; how we go about making social and political choices that shape how we act as citizens of our communities, our countries, and our planet. We all need these skills, and we need them like never before.

****

I've had the conversation a number of times, occasionally with actual leaders, but more commonly with people who are not leaders, about whether or not it is important for leaders to be intelligent. There are some who would argue that leaders don't need to be all that smart— they just need to have common sense, good "gut" instincts, and intelligent advisors.

Ironically, I rarely hear this from leaders who have been successful over the long term. Such leaders know that while they don't need to be the smartest person in the room in terms of, say, IQ, the best leaders have a pretty high baseline of general intelligence. Intelligence is needed because leaders have to be able to deal with greater complexity and think across longer time spans than does the average person. Leaders must have the raw cognitive horsepower to process the amount of information they encounter relative to their level of responsibility.

Does it help to have common sense? Sure, depending on what we mean by that term. If we mean the ability to learn from experience and develop practical judgment about real-world matters rather than abstractions, then yes, common sense is a good thing.

Unfortunately, however, people too often confuse common sense with the collection of prejudices referred to in the quote at the beginning of this article, or they confuse it with "naive intuition," the collection of cognitive biases and simplistic mental models that are part of the hard wiring of the human condition. (These biases and models will be covered in great detail in this series). They confuse this naïve intuition with the expert intuition that comes from long years of learning and practice and they often don't even realize there is a dramatic difference between the two.

Yes, the best leaders surround themselves with and rely on the advice of people who are smarter than they are, or who have relevant domain expertise in specific areas, but they also need the intelligence to be able to evaluate the advice given to them—to challenge, expand, and clarify when necessary.

And, yes, emotional intelligence (EQ) is important as well. Unfortunately, many misunderstand the literature on emotional intelligence and suggest that EQ is MORE important than IQ. What the literature on EQ actually says is that beyond a certain baseline of IQ, sufficient EQ will be more useful than additional IQ. The reality is that if one is not "intelligent enough" for the job, EQ—the ability to be aware of and manage emotional states in oneself and others— won't help that much.

The key phrase here is "intelligent enough." One must have higher intelligence to lead larger, more-complex organizations than to lead smaller, less-complex organizations, so "smart enough" varies from situation to situation. One might be intelligent enough for one leadership role but not intelligent enough for another.

However, one can be very intelligent but still make poor decisions and believe things that are pretty unbelievable (I know very intelligent people, for example, who actually believe the moon landings were faked).

So, the question of whether intelligence matters is a no-brainer—yes, it matters and it matters a lot. But, it's not enough. And the question becomes: Given that one has the requisite general intelligence for a particular role, are there intellectual qualities that separate those who will more-likely be successful from those who will more-likely stumble?

Yes, there are.

As I said, emotional intelligence helps. But I also believe that the ability to think effectively, to make the best use of one's innate intelligence and the knowledge, skills, and wisdom one has acquired—is one of the necessary keys to long-term success in leadership and in life. While it may not be possible to improve our innate general computing horsepower, we can get smarter by learning to think more effectively.

"Effective thinking" is, admittedly, a bit vague, so let me clarify what I mean by that. Effective thinking includes:

- Awareness of our innate biases and the tendencies of the human mind that undermine the accuracy of our perceptions.

- Critical-thinking skills, including a good "baloney detection kit."

- Curiosity about topics outside of one's domain of expertise and humility when acting within that domain.

- The use of rigorous tools and models for analysis and decision-making.

These qualities not only take us beyond common sense, they expose the flaws and inadequacies of our naïve common sense and help mitigate the dangers it can lead us into. They are also qualities that anyone can improve, no matter what their innate general intelligence is.

Naive Realism–Thinking We Know What is True

I have yet to meet the person who said, "Here's what I think, and I think I'm wrong." We have the views we do about the world around us because those views make sense to us. Whether it is something we have thought a lot about or whether we are following our initial gut reaction, everyone believes they believe what any reasonable person would believe given the same set of facts.

Psychologists call this phenomenon "naïve realism," which Thomas Gilovich and Lee Ross describe as "the seductive and compelling sense that one sees the world the way it is, not as a subjective take on the world" in their excellent new book, "The Wisest One in the Room."

As Gilovich and Ross point out, one of the functions of our brain is to make sense of the world and it has evolved numerous mechanisms to help us do so. They write: "Most of this sense making is done through mental processes that operate without our awareness, leaving us with the 'sense' but no awareness of the 'making.'… This lack of conscious access to our sense-making machinery leads to confusion between what Immanuel Kant called 'the thing as it is' and 'the thing as we know it.'"

Our brains manufacture certainty in a way that convinces us we interpret the world in a way that any "reasonable" person would, and we don't realize that much of what we believe is highly subjective ("the thing as we know it") and not necessarily a match to reality ("the thing as it is").

The importance of this simple idea cannot be overstated—we all think we are right about how we see the world and that anyone who thinks differently is either ill-informed or ill-intentioned. The greater the disparity between different points of view, and the more important a particular belief is to us, the more likely we are to attribute negative qualities to people who believe differently. The more you and I disagree on an important topic, the more likely you are to assume that I am not just stupid, but that I am a bad person as well. (And I will probably fall into the same trap…)

We see this in action in almost every walk of life—We may demonize people with other political or religious beliefs. We display contempt for supporters of rival sports teams. Even dog lovers and cat lovers can find themselves in hostile opposing camps. At work, simple disagreements about direction or priorities can lead to very personal feuds among individuals and broader schisms between whole groups of people. (When is the last time you heard people in Marketing speak positively about people in Engineering, or vice versa?)

Naive realism highlights the worst shortcomings of the kind of biased "common sense" we discussed in "Getting Smarter: Why Leaders Need to Be Better Thinkers.". Watching out for it and not falling victim to the traps of naive realism is the first step in moving "beyond common sense."

What To Do:

- Become a student of human nature and the cognitive biases that shape it. There are multiple reasons for our sense of certainty and the hostilities that can arise from it, and many will be discussed in this series. To understand them is to be armed against them.

- Recognize that everyone, even YOU, is a naïve realist and that you may well be mistaken, no matter how certain you feel about something.

- Give people the benefit of the doubt. You are victimized by naïve realism as much as they are, and your tendency to look down on or demonize people who hold different views is the result of non-conscious sense-making mechanism in your brain.

103

As we will see when we discuss the backfire effect, the best strategy to persuade others to your view is often taking a gentle and accepting approach. (By way of full disclosure, your author struggles mightily with this last one…:))

A Leader's Guide to How People Think (Part 1)

There is a scene in Clint Eastwood's movie "In the Line of Fire" where his character, Secret Service agent Frank Horrigan, is sitting on the steps of the Lincoln Memorial and trying to impress fellow agent Lilly Raines, played by Renee Russo. Frank makes a prediction about which of two pigeons will fly off first. Lilly, clearly dubious, says "How do you know?"

Frank grins and replies, "I know things about pigeons, Lilly."

Frank uses variations of this line in other parts of the movie, telling various characters that he "knows things about people," and the line is meant to capture something fundamental about Frank: Despite his sometimes-abrasive personality, he is really good at his job because he understands human nature and that understanding ultimately helps him stop an attempted assassination of the president.

Leaders, too, would do well to "know things about pigeons."

One of the primary responsibilities of leaders is to make good decisions and then influence others so they can see the wisdom of those decisions. Leaders are also responsible for deploying their subordinates— assigning them goals and tasks. Leaders will be better at these responsibilities if they understand how our minds work and the obstacles to clear thinking we put in our own way.

Figure 1 below shows a number of forces that can hinder our ability to think clearly and objectively, starting with embedded mechanisms in the brain at the bottom (the "bugs and features"), moving up through personality-related filters, culture, lack of information, and the embrace of misinformation. Figure 2 shows efforts we can make to overcome these forces. These diagrams are the foundation of Awareness to Action

International's "Critical Thinking for Leaders" program; this article takes a brief look at each level of the diagram.

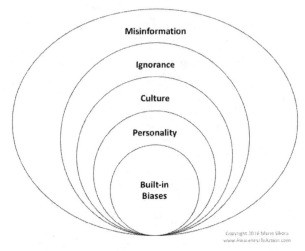

Figure 1: Forces that Can Shape Our Thinking

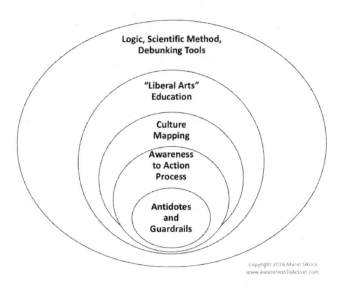

Figure 2: Ways to Overcome Obstacles to Clear Thinking

Built in Biases: The Mind's Features and Bugs

Our minds are a product of biological evolution and there are sophisticated and broad fields of evolutionary and cognitive psychology that go far beyond pop psychology and the notions that many leaders took in their Psych 101 course so many years ago. Here are some of the important concepts leaders should understand.

The Enigma of Reason and Self-Deception

The quote I probably throw around most frequently comes from the philosopher David Hume: "Truth springs from argument amongst friends." I believe it to be true in spirit, that the best way to get to an understanding of something is to throw out ideas and rigorously challenge them, preferably with other people; but I'm not sure Hume's statement is true in practice. Does argument—the act of reasoning with and against others—typically lead to truth?

As I write this, the US is in the midst of a seemingly endless presidential election process—the nominees have not yet been identified but it already seems like the campaign has been going on for years. Soon, candidates for each party will be chosen and in the run up to the election we will be treated to endless hours of interviews with their proxies arguing with each other on news talk shows. As in the past, they will argue with great force and passion and they will make very compelling arguments, but no one will change their mind.

These proxy debates are part of the pageantry of an election, and those watching the discussions will hear what they want to hear and go away convinced of what they were already convinced of. Argument rarely changes anyone's mind, let alone lead to truth; more frequently it ends up in a begrudging détente, an agreement to "agree to disagree."

This doesn't just happen in politics; it happens most times people debate or advocate for a point of view. We state our case clearly and expect the other person to say, "Hey, you are right and I was wrong," but much to our ongoing surprise they almost never do. It rarely occurs to us that the other person may be correct and that we should change our minds.

Take a moment to consider this. How many times have you argued with someone about something as important as an overall business strategy or a social issue, or about something relatively trivial such as who was the best quarterback or guitar player of all time? How often have you truly changed your mind based on someone else's argument? How often have the people you argued with changed their minds based on your reasoning?

As much as we like to think we are rational and evidence-based, most of our arguments are actually attempts to rationalize something that we intuitively *feel* is true and convince others of the merit of our intuitions.

Cognitive scientists Dan Sperber and Hugo Mercier have an explanation for this phenomenon that they call "the argumentative theory of reasoning," and we would do well to understand their ideas if we truly want to understand how our minds work. (They have written a book about this idea called "The Enigma of Reason.")

At the root of this theory, which is gaining traction with other cognitive scientists, is the idea that the brain did not evolve as a tool for accurate understanding of our world; it evolved to equip us to survive more effectively. They believe that all the cognitive biases (see "Critical Thinking: Tools for Leaders" in this collection) built into our minds are not glitches in the system, but features of the system that serve their purpose very effectively.

Survival requires getting the things we need and want from life, and we often do that more effectively when we can convince others to see the wisdom of our point of view (whether our point of view holds the actual truth or not...). Thus, our capacity to reason is not a tool for finding truth, or even for solving problems; our capacity to reason is a tool for convincing others of the rightness of our views so we can get what we want.

Further, Sperber and Mercier agree with cognitive scientists such as Robert Trivers, who makes the case in his book "The Folly of Fools," that the most effective way to convince others is to first fool ourselves into believing whatever story will justify our initial emotion-based intuitions. In short, we easily fool ourselves into believing convenient falsehoods that serve our selfish purposes, and then we reason skillfully for what we have fooled ourselves into believing. The more skilled we are at reasoning, the more we convince ourselves that those intuitions are correct.

People who reason skillfully are often able to convince others of their "rightness," frequently to the detriment of the one being convinced. Such people are what are commonly referred to as "influencers" and they often rise to leadership positions—with both positive and negative consequences.

Steve Jobs' legendary "reality distortion field" was one example of the argumentative theory of reasoning at work. Jobs was so convinced of the rightness of his vision that he was able to inspire himself and others to accomplish things no one thought possible. Our iPads and iPhones and the incredible success of Apple in general are examples of the positive outcomes of someone's ability to argue for his intuitions. Jobs' early death was the result of the darker side of this distortion—he was convinced he could ignore proper medical advice and be healed by "alternative" cures; his unwillingness or inability to listen to other points of view cost him his life.

The key implication of the argumentative theory of reasoning is that we can't always trust our own reasoning and we need objective, external tools to help us uncover the ways we may be deceiving ourselves. Sperber and Mercier also point out that the group needs objective methods to protect its members from charismatic, but wrong, leaders and influencers.

Simply adhering to what the boss says or following the most charismatic person in the room can be a recipe for disaster. The same thing that the great physicist Richard Feynman said about science applies to business as well: "it is important that you don't fool yourself, and you are the easiest person to fool."

This is where we return to Hume's statement—the way to find truth is to collaborate with others and "argue," but to do so deliberately, attentively, and with an open-mind. While we tend to think of arguing as the verbal combat that goes on nonstop on the news shows, Hume is actually calling for rational discourse—the joint pursuit of understanding rather than the competitive need for justification.

Other tools to protect the group from the compelling individual include the scientific method, social norms and mores, and institutions such as the church, schools, and government. While sometimes the individual is right and the group is wrong, we are well-served to have safeguards in check to protect ourselves from our ability to reason.

Since we are wired to deceive ourselves, we shouldn't demonize self-deception or when that self-deception in others leads them to inadvertently deceive others. Whenever possible, take the judgment out of the evaluation of points of view, and remember that when the stakes are higher people are more likely to deceive themselves. (Deliberate deception, of course, is unacceptable in the workplace.)

What you can do:

- Before we start to argue for our point of view we should take a deep breath, ask ourselves, "How do I know this to be true?" and argue against our own view.

- If you suspect you might be wrong, ask yourself, "What do I lose if find out I am wrong? Is it something small and ego-based? Or, is it something important, like a business deal or significant family matter?" If it's the former, use the opportunity to demonstrate humility and open-mindedness and let go of the errors of your ways. If the goal is genuinely important and can be achieved without harming others, ask "How can I accomplish my ultimate goals while acknowledging what is true?"

- It is important for leaders to establish effective group mechanisms for evaluating arguments in open and objective ways. Install a Devil's Advocate onto the team (this works best when the role is rotated so it doesn't fall on one person to always be the one arguing against the group). Run small tests on a premise and objectively measure the results. Reward, rather than marginalize, contrary thinking.

A Leader's Guide to How People Think (Part 2)

Cognitive Dissonance and Cognitive Biases

"The test of a first-rate intelligence is the ability to hold two opposed ideas in mind at the same time and still retain the ability to function."
F. Scott Fitzgerald

Cognitive Dissonance

Cognitive dissonance is the tension caused by contradictory ideas battling for space in the psyche. Such tension causes us stress and anxiety, so our mind seeks to dispel it as quickly as possible. It does so by finding a way to reject one of the ideas without due consideration, preferably the one that contradicts our currently held beliefs.

The root of cognitive dissonance is in our attempt to maintain our self-esteem. We all want to think well of ourselves. Few of us see ourselves as bad people, even if we sometimes make mistakes. When we do something that contradicts our perception of ourselves, we experience the discomfort of cognitive dissonance. We then fall victim to a variety of cognitive biases—such as the confirmation bias—automatic mental models that can distort our thinking. Embracing these biases is the brain's way of dispelling that tension and protecting our positive view of ourselves.

For example, if we think we are doing well in our role and we get negative feedback in a 360 assessment, it is tempting to rationalize the feedback by attributing ignorance or malice to the source of the comments we don't like, or to assume that the comments are based on insufficient or flawed data. If we design a product we truly believe in but it is not well-received by the market, it is tempting to blame the users or believe that our product is "too ahead of its time" rather than think there might be something wrong with the product.

While cognitive dissonance affects all of us in many aspects of our lives, it is particularly important for leaders to be aware of this phenomenon. Cognitive dissonance, and our non-conscious attempts to dispel it, is what cause us to fail hear or appropriately consider other points of view. The more pressure we feel to be right or appear confident, the more we can fall victim to this tendency. Leaders simply cannot afford to not adequately consider other points of view so they must be skilled at spotting cognitive dissonance and its affects in themselves and others.

It is helpful to understand that cognitive dissonance and our attempts to mitigate it happen below the level of our awareness—we don't do it on purpose. Our mind identifies tension before we consciously register it and sets us on the course of some process to make it go away by applying a cognitive bias. We all do it, and we don't realize it. We don't do it because we are bad people, it happens unless we train ourselves to look for signs of cognitive dissonance (such as, the stress we feel when confronted with an idea we don't like) and take steps to avoid falling into the traps of our mitigating biases. Such training is how we achieve the "first-rate intelligence" Fitzgerald wrote of.

What to Do About Cognitive Dissonance:

- Learn to look for cognitive dissonance in yourself—the internal stress when feedback or observations rub you the wrong way for reasons you can't quite identify.

- Learn to observe cognitive dissonance in others without judgment—seeing it in action can help us see it earlier in ourselves.

- Avoid the temptation to flatly reject ideas that don't fit your worldview. Explore, with an open mind, ideas you are tempted to flatly reject.

- Avoid either/or thinking—the giver of feedback may be biased AND you may still have the flaws he identified; the product may be ahead of its time AND it may still have some flaws, etc.

Cognitive Biases

We tend to assume that attractive people are also smart; we assume that when we make a mistake it is due to circumstances but when others make a mistake it is because they have some character defect; we recognize evidence that supports our beliefs far more easily than evidence that contradicts them; we tend to inflate our role and minimize the role of others when describing an event.

These are all examples of cognitive biases—distortions of perception and analysis—that we unconsciously use to argue for our intuitive point of view or system of beliefs. Cognitive biases are shortcuts in thinking—they are useful in providing mental shortcuts that save our brain time and energy, but may also distort our perception of reality. They also serve as a way of dispelling cognitive dissonance—easing the tension that conflicting ideas or feelings can cause. This resolution of cognitive dissonance is not always a positive thing because it can mean

Understanding cognitive biases and being able to recognize when we or others fall victim to them is a fundamental skill in the critical thinker's tool kit. Charlie Munger, Warren Buffet's lesser-known partner in Berkshire Hathaway, places great value on understanding cognitive biases and how they affect business and financial decisions. His writings on them are a central part of "Poor Charlie's Almanac," a compendium of his articles and speeches.

Confirmation Bias

Confirmation bias is among the most basic and insidious of the cognitive biases. It refers to the tendency we all have to see what we want to see or what we expect to see. It is the tendency to embrace evidence that fits our point of view (referred to as *biased assimilation*) and to ignore or minimize evidence that does not fit (referred to as *cognitive discounting*).

It is important to understand that confirmation bias occurs without our awareness. We don't do it because we are bad, ill-intentioned, or lazy; we do it without realizing we are doing it. It is one of the mind's favorite ways of relieving the stress of cognitive dissonance.

Confirmation bias is what causes us to be overly optimistic about projects, products, or people.

If we have an investment in the success of a project, we will find all the reasons we can for why it will be successful and ignore obstacles to its completion.

If we believe in a product we are developing, we will find plenty of evidence that there is a huge market for it.

If we think one of our employees is a rising star, we will only see what he does well and overlook warning signs of trouble.

At the same time, confirmation bias can make us ignore evidence of signals that we should pay more attention to something we are dismissing.

We may miss disruptive competitive products in the market because all we can see is the evidence of how superior our product is.

When assessing employees we can fixate on the evidence that reinforces our negative opinion of someone rather than seeing all the progress she has made in her development.

Confirmation bias is a constant threat to clear and effective thinking. The best thinkers safeguard themselves by asking some simple questions: How do I know this to be true? What evidence is there that I could be wrong? They also take pride in changing their mind based on new evidence.

For more cognitive biases, see the article "Critical Thinking: Tools for Leaders" in this collection.

A Leader's Guide to How People Think (Part 3)

Personality, Culture, Ignorance, Error

Personality-Driven Focus of Attention

Layered above the bugs and features of our cognitive system described in Part 2, our personality style influences how we think and view the world. People with different personality styles pay attention to different things and place value on different things.

If our personality styles are different, you will focus on some things and I will focus on others. You will value some ways of thinking, feeling, and behaving; I will value others. These differences are not inherently bad; in fact, we can't all focus on everything so personality differences are one way of raising a group's level of competence. I can be good at this and you can be good at that, and if we work together we are good at two things instead of being mediocre at everything.

People fall into personality patterns because the brain likes to habituate behaviors that appear to work. Our brains use about 20% of our body's energy and is always looking for ways to reduce that load. Therefore, we have evolved as cognitive misers and our brains tend to find short cuts by creating habits. These habits allow us to run on autopilot much of the time. Our collection of habits of thinking, feeling, and acting are the root of our personality style

My preferred model of personality styles is the Enneagram, which identifies three clusters of instinctual values and nine strategies for satisfying those values. See the articles on the Enneagram model in the beginning of this collection for much more information on this system. I also think there is value in the Big Five model, which explores a person's level of extroversion, agreeableness, conscientiousness, neuroticism, and openness to experience.

A note about personality models: Personality models are "heuristics" shorthand mental models that help us simplify complex creatures. They should be used as such—tools to understand and enlighten, not weapons to minimize and stereotype. In my nearly 20 years of working with leaders I have seen leaders of all personality styles who were very successful and leaders of all styles who failed. There is no ideal personality style for success in any role. Using a personality model to stereotype someone is to fall victim to the "correspondence bias," a cognitive bias that causes us to make broad but short-sighted generalizations about others based on a few observed traits.

The value of personality models is to help us see our own habitual patterns so we can minimize the damage they do and to understand that others are just as trapped in their habitual patterns as we are so that we can be more sympathetic to them. This sympathy allows us to interact with them in ways that will speak to their values rather than in ways that speak to ours. This dramatically increases the chances of successful communication and collaboration.

Culture

We are becoming ever-more globalized. While most of our ancestors often rarely encounter anyone outside the tribe or strayed far from their homes, we live in an age where we can board an airplane and be almost anywhere in the world the next day. It is an age of multinational organizations and multi-lingual people, and there is a good chance that most of your possessions where made somewhere far away. This means that understanding culture grows more important every day.

One way of understanding "culture" is to see it as a given group's implicitly or explicitly agreed-upon way of solving the problems of group living. Culture is the source of most human accomplishment; it is the source of our shared sense of meaning, accountability, and responsibilities; it is what allows us to survive together. The downside of culture is that it can provide another filter that makes it difficult to see objectively.

Culture can shape many aspects of how we interpret the world.

Culture can shape our relationship with time—people some cultures live in "clock time" ("The bus will be here at 10:20 am"), others are live in "event time" ("Don't worry, the bus will get here when it gets here").

Other differences in culture include:

- *Collectivist* ("The well-being of the group is what matters most") vs *individualist* ("The well-being of the individual is what matters most"),
- *Assertive* ("Here is what I can do") vs *humble* ("I did not do much"),
- *Low Uncertainty Avoidance* ("Whatever happens will happen; new things are opportunities") vs *High Uncertainty Avoidance* ("We have to make efforts ensure that bad things don't happen; new things are threats."),
- *Short-term view* ("We need to worry about what is happening now") vs long-term view ("We have to worry about what will happen in the future"), and
- *Small-power distance* ("The powerful are responsible to the masses") and large-power distance ("The masses must obey the powerful").

Each culture exists somewhere on a continuum in each of these areas, and each culture has its own unique profile. People from cultures with similar characteristics find it easier to connect with each other; the more different our cultures are, the more foreign we will feel to each other.

Leaders, particularly those whose responsibilities span multiple cultural groups, would do well to familiarize themselves with these differences and learn to embrace them.

Lack of Knowledge (Ignorance)

A person's knowledge and experience shapes their worldview, and their worldview shapes how they think about the world around them. A person who has a broader range of knowledge and life experiences will generally have a broader perspective. Someone with a narrower range of knowledge and experiences will have a narrower perspective. There is always a trade-off between specialization and breadth, but what separates the best thinkers from the rest is curiosity.

Unfortunately, most people aren't that curious. As we have already seen, the brain likes to create habits and stick within its comfort zone of habitual thoughts whenever possible. Exposing ourselves to new information and other perspectives can seem threatening to that comfort. As we've also seen, the brain likes to filter out information that doesn't fit our existing mental models.

The result is that many people end up not pursuing new knowledge and filtering out alternative perspectives without realizing it. The result— we don't know as much as we think we do.

There is even a name for this—the Dunning-Kruger Effect. Psychologists David Dunning and Justin Kruger studied expertise and found that people with less expertise in a topic tend to overestimate their knowledge while people with more expertise tend to underestimate their knowledge. Since we tend to overestimate our knowledge of a given topic, it is very easy to stop working to learn more.

The real-world result of this is that we miss opportunities of all sorts. People with more knowledge and experience are able to see nuance, context, and connection much better than those with less. Ignorance can make us miss business opportunities, keep us from improving our products, and keep us from improving ourselves.

Leaders do well to build a culture of continual learning in their organization. Be sure to reward curiosity and experimentation. Create a "liberal arts" mindset" where people are encouraged to learn outside of their scope of responsibility.

For tips on developing such a mindset, see the article "Leadership as A Liberal Art: A Reading List for Leaders" in this collection

Misinformation

Perhaps even more dangerous than ignorance—not knowing something that is true—is being misinformed and believing things that are not true. The challenge of living in the so-called "Post-Truth" Information Age is that not all information is created equal—it often seems we are exposed to as much bunk as we are to actual facts. For example, it is easier to find information telling us that vaccines or GMOs are dangerous (they are not) than it is to find solid science. (Fortunately, Google is trying to address this and other topics prone to misinformation by adjusting its algorithms.)

Mark Twain famously said that "a lie can get halfway around the world before the truth gets its boots on." And while he "famously" said it, he didn't actually say it—this quote is in itself a great example of misinformation. No one knows who said this first but it predates Twain by at least a century and it is not included in any of his writings (or so I've read…hmmm…). This is just one simple example of the flood of misinformation we are deluged with when we step onto the information super-highway.

It is difficult to protect ourselves. It is easy to accept the quote as original because it feels right. "Genetically modified organisms" sound like dangerous things, so it is easy to accept the misinformation that they are. Few of us have the time to debunk quotes or research genetic engineering or any of the other topics we are faced with but expected to have an opinion on. So we embrace what feels true.

There are two cognitive biases that reinforce our embrace of misinformation: biased assimilation and belief polarization.

Biased assimilation is the aspect of the confirmation bias that inclines us to embrace information that conforms to our existing beliefs. Again, the brain likes habits and this applies to ideas that fit an existing groove in our gray matter.

Belief polarization is what happens when people are confronted with information that contradicts their beliefs—no matter how good the argument or clear the facts, people are more prone to end up even more convinced of their existing beliefs when they are they are confronted with contradictory evidence. In other words, the more you try to convince someone of the errors of their beliefs, the more entrenched in those beliefs they will become.

Finally, we tend to live in echo chambers—surrounded by people who think like we do and are all too happy to tell us how correct we are. We attend conferences filled with people from our business or academic fields. We watch news channels or read editorial pages that reinforce our political views. We join clubs made up of people with the same socio-economic background. All of these things become part of our intrinsic identity and stepping outside of them can feel very threatening, so we tend not to do it. This leaves us vulnerable to not only missing the opportunity to learn new things, but vulnerable to accepting misinformation.

Logic and Logic Fallacies

Given the challenges already stated, it is easy to see that we are not innately logical creatures. In fact, our intuitions, cognitive biases, and emotions can often undermine logic and lead us into logical fallacies. Learning to identify logical fallacies is one way to help ensure that we don't fall victim to misinformation.

Logic is a skill, and is very different from "common sense." Einstein identified "common sense" as "the collection of prejudices we acquire by the age of 18." Everyone thinks they have common sense and that most other people lack it, which should be the signal of a problem with the concept right away. Logic requires training and education, and leaders would do well to acquire it.

There are many interesting ways to learn about logical fallacies online, and some sources are listed at the end of this article. It helps to know that logical fallacies come in two forms: formal and informal.

Formal fallacies are marked by a factual or structural flaw in the argument. An example is: All dogs are mortal. Mittens is mortal. Therefore, Mittens is a dog. Even though both premises are true, the conclusion does not follow from the premises if we also know that Mittens is actually a cat.

Informal fallacies are often more subtle and nuanced, and frequently the result of the conflation, or the mixing up of, our thinking, naïve intuitions, and cognitive biases. Thus, arguments often hold appeal to our emotions and seem intuitively correct even if they don't withstand scrutiny.

An informal fallacy does not necessarily invalidate a conclusion, but it calls the conclusion into question and points to the need for additional analysis.

A good example of this is the post hoc, ergo propter hoc fallacy. This is Latin for "after the thing, therefore because of the thing." I recently overheard someone saying that he would never get the flu shot again because: "I never had the flu or got a flu shot before last year. But then I got the flu shot and I got the flu shortly. Therefore, the flu shot caused the flu."

The flaw is thinking that just because he got the flu after he got the shot, the shot caused the flu. Since it well-known scientifically that the flu shot does not cause the flu, it is far more likely that he contracted a strain of flu for which the vaccine was not effective. It is also likely that since he got the flu shot at the beginning of the flu shot, the timing was a coincidence.

Awareness of the post hoc fallacy helps us separate true causes of events from the noise. Understanding other fallacies—argument from authority, argument from antiquity, *tu quoque*, the sharpshooter fallacy, etc.—can be equally useful.

Recognizing the value of expert intuition, emotion, and gut feeling are important, but nothing beats cold, hard logic applied at the right time. A rule of thumb is that when it comes to linear problems, logic rules. When it comes to complex problems, do all your factual due-diligence; apply logic; correct for logical fallacies, cognitive biases, and personality biases; then trust your belly.

For a list of common logical fallacies and other tools for identifying misinformation, see "Critical Thinking: Tools for Leaders" in this collection.

Conclusion

We all like to think that we see the world clearly and that other people see it as clearly as we do. The truth is that we each have our own unique set of filters and distortions that shape the way we see the world. While it is impossible for leaders to truly understand the unique psychology of everyone they lead, understanding the broad variables that shape our minds is a great advantage for leaders who want to effectively influence, persuade, and inspire them.

Critical Thinking: Tools for Leaders

By Mario Sikora

The ability to think clearly relies partly on attitude and partly on having the requisite skills and tools.

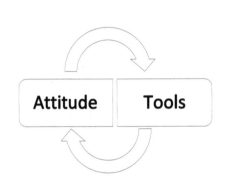

The attitude required for critical is skepticism.

Skepticism is the attitude and practice of matching the evidence to the claim. It assumes both an open mind and a critical mind. It is a willingness to hear the other side of an argument and to change one's mind if a compelling enough argument is made, while still being committed to rigorously challenging assumptions.

Skepticism is different from *cynicism*, which has come to mean the automatic dismissal of the new or strange. While cynicism starts with a closed mind, skepticism starts with an open mind and a clear-eyed willingness to question even one's own most cherished beliefs and assumptions.

The patron saint of skepticism is the Scottish enlightenment philosopher David Hume, who asserted that we really can't KNOW anything for sure but that a "wise man [or woman] proportions his belief to the evidence." The late scientist and educator Carl Sagan popularized a version of Hume's statement as "extraordinary claims require extraordinary evidence."

Skepticism begins with assessing the plausibility of a claim—given what we already know, how likely is it that a particular claim is true? The more implausible a claim is, the more evidence we should require (and the more rigorous we should be in evaluating the validity of that evidence). Further, the consequences of a claim affect the amount of evidence we should require.

For example, if someone tells me she owns a golden retriever and shows me a picture of herself with a golden retriever, I don't need a lot of evidence to provisionally believe her. If I know she has a tendency to lie, I may hold some doubt, but it is not implausible that someone owns a golden retriever. And since the consequences related to whether or not she owns a golden retriever are minimal, I would not feel the need to seek a lot of evidence to support her claim.

If, however, someone tells me they can cure cancer by waving their healing hands over a person, I would require a lot of evidence. Such a claim is highly implausible given what we know about cancer, and the consequences of someone seeking "healing hands" treatment for cancer are dire.

If we want to be good critical thinkers and claim to be seekers after truth, we should cultivate appropriate skepticism and remember Carl Sagan's other famous quote: *"It pays to keep an open mind, but not so open that your brains fall out."*

Once the right attitude is in place, some fundamental tools are helpful; the rest of this article provides some of those tools.

The Critical-Thinking Framework

The Critical-Thinking Framework is a model for analyzing a situation or assertion. It is a list of questions that should be answered when pressure-testing any idea or argument. Not all of them will apply to every situation, but it provides a good checklist. While I recommend people use it as a literal checklist in the beginning, once you gain some familiarity with the list you will find yourself asking the questions intuitively. Both it and the Assumption Analysis Questionnaire that follow are adapted from the book "Red Teaming," by Bryce G. Hoffman.

1. What are the key issues and the conclusions drawn about them?
   a. Does the argument being made address a relevant problem?
2. What are the reasons given in support of the conclusions?
   a. Does the rational support the conclusion?
   b. What are the leaps of assumption that need to be challenged?
3. What words, phrases, or concepts used are unclear, vague, or ambiguous?
   a. Is the advocate willing to clarify them?
4. What are the implicit (or explicit) value assumptions or conflicts?
   a. Can the advocate satisfactorily justify them?
5. What are the implicit (or explicit) descriptive assumptions?
   a. Does the advocate describe either the presence or absence of characteristics in a way that is not supported by the facts?
   b. Does the advocate make any unsupported assumptions about the way things *should* be?
   c. Is there any bias in the intention of the argument or the description of the situation? What is the bias and how might it be shaping the argument?
6. How robust and relevant is the evidence?
   a. What, if any, are the logical fallacies affecting the validity of the argument?
7. Are their rival or alternative explanations for the causes?
8. Are the statistics vague, relevant, or deceptive?
9. What important information is ignored?
10. What reasonable conclusion is possible?

Assumption Analysis Questionnaire

The Critical-Thinking Framework applies for analyzing broader arguments; the Assumption Analysis Questionnaire is for analyzing specific assumptions that may or may not be part of a larger argument. Both tools can be applied to our own assumptions and arguments or those presented to us by others.

The Assumption Analysis Questionnaire is:

1. Is this logical? (See list of logical fallacies below.)
2. Is this accurate?
3. Is this based on preconceived notions or biases? (See list of cognitive biases below.)
4. Is this based on historical analogies, and if so, are they relevant?
5. What has to happen for this to become true?
6. How much confidence do the planners have that this will happen?
7. If this becomes true, will it remain true under all conditions?
8. If this proves to be untrue, how would that alter the plan?

Recognizing Cognitive Biases

Cognitive biases, as described in the article "A Leader's Guide to How People Think" in this collection, are mental shortcuts that save the brain time and energy but can lead to inaccuracy. The occur without our awareness and we all fall victim to them. The first step in protecting ourselves from their detrimental effects is to be aware of them.

Below is a list of common biases *(the definitions are adapted from Wikipedia.org)*. For further information on cognitive biases, refer to any of the following books: "Thinking, Fast and Slow," by Daniel Kahneman; "The Undoing Project," by Michael Lewis; "The Wisest One in the Room" by Thomas Gilovich and Lee Ross.

- *Affect heuristic:* a mental shortcut in which current emotion—fear, pleasure, surprise, etc.—influences decisions.

- *Anchoring or focalism:* the tendency to rely too heavily on the first piece of information offered (the "anchor") when making decisions.

- *Automation bias:* the propensity for humans to over-rely on suggestions from automated decision-making systems.

- *Availability heuristic:* the tendency to rely on immediate examples that come to mind when evaluating a situation or decision. Overvalues things that can be recalled easily, even if they are less accurate or useful pieces of data than things that are less easy to recall.

- *Bandwagon effect:* the tendency to embrace ideas, beliefs, fads or trends that are popular with others.

- *Clustering illusion:* the tendency to see random clustering in a small sample as a pattern reflecting a larger trend.

- *Confirmation bias:* is the tendency to non-consciously embrace or interpret information in a way that confirms one's preexisting beliefs or hypotheses.

- *Curse of knowledge:* the tendency of experts to overestimate an audience's or another person's depth of knowledge of a given topic.

- *Escalation of commitment:* when an individual or group—faced with increasingly negative outcomes from some decision, action, or investment—continues the same behavior rather than change course.

- *Framing effect:* the tendency of the presentation method of the information to shape the perception of the information.

- *Gambler's fallacy:* the belief that if something happens more frequently than normal during a given period it will happen less frequently in the future, or vice versa.

- *Halo effect:* when an observer's overall impression of a person, company, brand, or product influences the observer's feelings and thoughts about that entity's character or specific properties. The tendency to assume higher competence among more-attractive people is a good example.

- *Hindsight bias:* the tendency, after an event has occurred, to unjustifiably see the event as having been predictable.

- *Illusion of control:* the tendency for people to overestimate their ability to control events.

- *Loss aversion:* the tendency to significantly prefer avoiding losses to acquiring equivalent gains.

- *Negativity bias:* the tendency of negative experiences to have a substantially greater impact on people's perceptions than neutral or positive experiences.

- *Normalcy bias:* the tendency to underestimate the possibility of disasters and minimize their potential impact, assuming that things will function basically like they always have. Leads to a lack of planning for emergencies.

- *Optimism bias:* the belief that the individual is at less risk of experiencing negative events than others are.

- *Ostrich effect:* the tendency to avoid bad news; especially when related to finances.

- *Outcome bias:* an error made when evaluating the quality of a decision when the outcome of that decision is already known.

- *Overconfidence effect:* when a person's subjective *confidence* in his or her judgments is reliably greater than the objective *accuracy* of those judgements, especially when confidence is relatively high. Similar to *Dunning-Kruger effect* in which people who are less competent tend to over-rate their competence and people who are more competent tend to underrate their competence.

- *Planning fallacy:* the tendency to underestimate the time and effort needed to complete a future task.

- *Regression fallacy:* the assumption that circumstances returned to normal (regression to the mean) due to corrective actions taken rather than natural fluctuations.

- *Selective memory:* the brain's tendency to select, delete, or distort memories without our awareness.

- *Status quo bias:* a preference for the current state of affairs, and tendency to use the status quo as the baseline reference point despite longer term trends that demonstrate otherwise.

- *Sunk cost fallacy:* an unwillingness or resistance to cut one's losses, even in the face of evidence that further investment will lead to greater loss.

- *Temporal discounting:* the tendency of people to discount rewards when they are farther in the future or the past.

Logical Fallacies

Given the challenges already stated, it is easy to see that we are not inherently logical creatures. In fact, our intuitions, cognitive biases, and emotions can often undermine logic and lead us into logical fallacies.

Logic is a skill, and is very different from "common sense." Einstein identified "common sense" as "the collection of prejudices we acquire by the age of 18." Everyone thinks they have common sense and that most other people lack it, which should be the signal of a problem with the concept right away. Logic requires training and education.

There are many interesting ways to learn about logical fallacies online, and some sources are listed at the end of this article. It helps to know that logical fallacies come in two forms: formal and informal.

Formal fallacies are marked by a factual or structural flaw in the argument. An example is: All dogs are mortal. Mittens is mortal. Therefore, Mittens is a dog. Even though both premises are true, the conclusion does not follow from the premises if we also know that Mittens is actually a cat.

Informal fallacies are often more subtle and nuanced, and frequently the result of the conflation, or the mixing up of, our thinking, naïve intuitions, and cognitive biases. Thus, arguments often hold appeal to our emotions and seem intuitively correct even if they don't withstand scrutiny.

An informal fallacy does not necessarily invalidate a conclusion, but it calls the conclusion into question and points to the need for additional analysis.

A good example of this is the post hoc, ergo propter hoc fallacy. This is Latin for "after the thing, therefore because of the thing." I recently overheard someone saying that he would never get the flu shot again because: "I never had the flu or got a flu shot before last year. But then I got the flu shot and I got the flu shortly. So the flu shot caused the flu."

The flaw is thinking that just because he got the flu after he got the shot, the shot caused the flu. Since it well-established that the flu shot does not cause the flu, it is far more likely that he contracted a strain of flu for which the vaccine was not effective. It is also likely that since he got the flu shot at the beginning of the flu season, the timing was a coincidence.

Common Logical Fallacies:

- *Ad hominem:* attacking the person rather than the merit of the idea they are proposing.

- *Appeal to antiquity or custom:* giving undue validity to an argument because it is old or part of a tradition.

- *Appeal to authority:* giving undue validity to an argument because an important or famous person made it.

- *Appeal to emotion:* encouraging people to focus on their feelings rather than the facts when evaluating an argument.

- *Appeal to popularity:* claiming that an argument is valid because a lot of people believe it.

- *Appeal to the stone:* dismissing a claim as absurd without providing proof for its absurdity.

- *Argument from ignorance:* assuming that a claim is true because it has not been or cannot be proven false, or vice versa.

- *Argument from incredulity:* "I cannot imagine how this could be true; therefore, it must be false."

- *Begging the question:* providing the conclusion of the argument as a premise.

- *Shifting the burden of proof:* I need not prove my claim, you must prove it is false.

- *Circular reasoning:* when the reasoner begins with what he or she is trying to end up with; sometimes called *assuming the conclusion.*

- *Circular cause and consequence:* when the consequence of the phenomenon is claimed to be its root cause.

- *Correlation proves causation (post hoc ergo propter hoc* "after the thing, therefore because of the thing"): a flawed assumption that because there is a correlation between two variables that one caused the other.

- *False authority:* elevating an expert of dubious credentials or using only one opinion to promote a product or idea.

- *False choice:* when two contrasting statements are held to be the only possible options when in reality there are more.

- *False equivalence:* assuming logical and apparent equivalence when in fact there is none.

- *Fallacy of the single cause:* assuming there is one simple cause of an outcome when in it may have actually been caused by a number of interrelated causes.

- *Inflation of conflict:* assuming that if experts disagree on a certain point, the scholars of a whole field must not know anything.

- *McNamara fallacy (quantitative fallacy):* making a decision based only on quantitative observations and discounting all other considerations.

- *Moving the goalposts:* an argument in which the evidence presented in response to a specific claim is dismissed with a demand for some other (often greater) evidence.

- *Naturalistic fallacy:* inferring the something is good because it is the way it is now or it is the way it was in the past.

- *Shifting the burden of proof:* assuming that the person questioning a claim is responsible for proving the validity of the claim, rather than assuming the burden is on the person making the claim.

- *Proof by assertion:* repeatedly restating a proposition regardless of contradiction.

- *Proof by verbosity*: overwhelming others with an argument too complex and verbose to reasonably deal with in all its details.

- *Prosecutor's fallacy:* a low probability of false matches does not mean a low probability of *some* false match being found.

- *Psychologist's fallacy:* presupposes the objectivity of one's own perspective when analyzing a behavioral event.

- *Red herring:* an attempt to distract an audience by deviating from the topic at hand with a separate argument the speaker believes is easier to address.

- *Reification:* when an abstraction is treated as if it were a concrete, real event or physical entity.

- *Shotgun argumentation:* the arguer offers such a large number of arguments for a position that the opponent can't possibly respond to all of them.

- *Special pleading:* when an advocate of a position attempts to cite an exemption to a generally accepted rule or principle without justifying the exemption.

Other Tools:

Occam's Razor

Named after medieval philosophe William of Ockham, Occam's Razor is another name for the *principle of parsimony*—the principle that we should keep explanations as simple as possible (but no simpler!) Commonly misunderstood as meaning that the simplest answer is usually the correct answer, Occam's Razor actually encourages us to not add factors unnecessarily. If we can adequately explain a phenomenon with two factors, we shouldn't add a third.

For example, if we want to explain how ice forms, the first equation below is better than the second.

$$\boxed{\checkmark}\ \text{Ice} = \text{Water} + \text{Cold}$$

$$\boxed{\times}\ \ \text{Ice} = \text{Water} + \text{Cold} + \text{Ice-making fairies}$$

Avoid Unjustified Leaps of Inference

An unjustified leap of inference is drawing a conclusion that may not necessarily flow from the premises used to arrive at that conclusion. For example, just because I can safely jump off a curb and jump off a chair does not mean I can safely jump off a cliff. Assuming I *could* do so would be a leap too far.

Leaps of inference are far more common than we realize. They are often the root of conspiracy thinking or questionable assertions about history or science. They are a mechanism that allows us to embrace beliefs we *want* to believe but for which we don't have solid evidence.

It is important to examine every assumption in our argument or perspective and make sure that it is justified by the evidence or logic that came before it.

Learn to Distinguish Between Naïve Intuition and Expert Intuition

System 1 thinking inclines us to trust our intuition, even if our intuition is not accurate. There is a distinct difference between naïve intuition— intuition that is based on uninformed "gut" feelings—and skilled intuition—the kind of non-conscious expertise that is the result of extensive training and experience.

If you've ever seriously studied or trained in a physical, artistic, or even intellectual pursuit, you know that after a lot of practice things that initially seemed difficult and required a lot of conscious effort became intuitive and automatic after time. This is because you trained your mind and your muscles to non-consciously act, but these actions were based on practiced expertise.

The challenge we have is that the mind cannot always tell the difference between the feeling of this kind of skillful expertise and the illusory feeling of expertise in an area in which we have no trained competence. For example, because we develop the capacity to intuitively read the emotions and moods of people we know well based on repeated experience, we tend to falsely believe we can intuit the moods and needs of people we have just met. This same phenomenon is found in many areas.

Intuition is a useful and critical part of our nature, but we have to remember that there is a difference between skillful intuition based on experience and practice and potentially dangerous naïve intuition based on nothing but a false feeling of competence.

Recommended Resources for Critical Thinking and How the Mind Works:

Bibliography

Argumentative Theory of Reasoning:

- Sperber, Dan, and Hugo Mercier, "The Enigma of Reason"

- "The Argumentative Theory—A Conversation with Hugo Mercier," http://edge.org/conversation/hugo_mercier-the-argumentative-theory

- Sperber, Dan and Hugo Mercier, "Why Do Humans Reason? Arguments for an Argumentative Theory," https://hal.archives-ouvertes.fr/hal-00904097/document.

Self-Deception:

- Trivers, Robert, "The Folly of Fools"

- Galinsky, Adam and Maurice Schweitzer, "Friend & Foe: When to Cooperate, When to Compete, and How to Succeed at Both."

Cognitive Dissonance:

- Tavris, Carol and Elliot Aronson, "Mistakes Were Made (but not by me): Why We Justify Foolish Beliefs, Bad Decisions, and Hurtful Acts."

Cognitive Biases:

- Daniel Kahneman, "Thinking Fast and Slow"

- Wood, Jennifer, "20 Cognitive Biases That Affect Your Decisions," http://mentalfloss.com/us/go/68705

- Wilke, A and R Mata, "Cognitive Bias," The Encyclopedia of Human Behavior, http://people.clarkson.edu/~awilke/Research_files/Eo HB_Wilke_12.pdf

Personality Styles

- Tallon, Robert and Mario Sikora, "Awareness to Action: The Enneagram, Emotional Intelligence, and Change."

- Barondes, Samuel, "Making Sense of People: Decoding the Mysteries of Personality"

Culture

- Trompenaars, Fons, and Charles Hampden-Turner, "Riding the Waves of Culture"

- Cabrera, Angel, and Gregory Unruh, "Being Global: How to Think, Act, and Lead in a Transformed World"

- Hofstede, Geert, and Gert Jan Hofstede, "Cultures and Organizations: Software of the Mind"

Knowledge

- Grazer, Brian and Charles Fishman, "A Curious Mind"

- Steves, Rick, "Travel as a Political Act"

- Bazerman, Max, "The Power of Noticing."

Misinformation

- Ellenberg, Jordan, "How Not to Be Wrong: The Power of Mathematical Thinking."

- Pigliucci, Massimo, "Nonsense on Stilts: How to Tell Science from Bunk."

- Mitroff, Ian I., and Warren Bennis, "The Unreality Industry: The Deliberate Manufacturing of Falsehood and What it is Doing to our Lives."

- Thompson, Damian, "Counterknowledge: How we surrendered to conspiracy theories, quack medicine, bogus science, and fake history."

- Huff, Darrell, "How to Lie With Statistics."

- Gardner, Martin, "Science: Good, Bad, and Bogus"

Logic and Logical Fallacies:

- DiCarlo, Christopher, "How to Become a Really Good Pain in the A**"

- "Your Logical Fallacy Is" website, yourlogicalfallacyis.com.

- "Master List of Logical Fallacies," http://utminers.utep.edu/omwilliamson/ENGL1311/fallacies.htm.

141

Post-Mortems and Pre-Mortems–Learning from the Past and Learning from the Future

As 2015 draws to a close and 2016 quickly approaches, it's a great opportunity to take stock and think about what just happened and what is about to happen. And, it's a great time to think about how best to prepare for the latter.

But first, let's take some time to celebrate. "Celebrate" is not usually a word associated with "post-mortem," which is an examination that seeks to find the cause of a thing's demise. Yes, it helps to look back and see what went wrong and what we could have done better, and we should do this. However, this is also a time to recognize and celebrate our successes–goals accomplished and what particular actions or capabilities we contributed in helping to accomplish those goals.

It is common practice in the military to conduct an "after-action analysis." A squad goes on a mission and when they come back they spend time rigorously identifying what went well, what could have gone better, and what steps they can take to enhance their understanding of best practices and ensure that missions go better in the future.

I encourage my clients to conduct such after-action analyses as a practice for tracking growth in a developmental area they have identified. If they are working on communicating more effectively with their boss, for example, I encourage them to take a few minutes after each conversation with their boss and ask, "What went well? What didn't go well? What should I do again next time? What could I do differently next time?"

This is not rocket science–these questions are very basic and obvious. The problem is that we usually don't ask them. We are so focused on what we have to do next that we don't take a moment to think about what just happened and how we can learn from it. And because we don't take these few simple minutes, we don't improve.

The same process can be applied to the past year. Take a little time and ask yourself some simple questions:

- What did I do well, and how can I do those things again in the future?

- What didn't go so well and how can I avoid that happening again?

It is important, however, to really pay attention to the first question and to celebrate your successes. High-achieving people tend to be successful because they are always looking for ways to improve and overcome their weaknesses. They forget to acknowledge their strengths and accomplishments. The downside to this is that they miss the opportunity to strategically leverage their strengths in the future.

Taking a moment to celebrate our strengths feeds the reward system in the brain and increases the chance that we will repeat those behaviors without having to really think about it. The celebration may seem gratuitous to you, but do it as an investment in increasing the likelihood of future success.

Future success is not guaranteed, however. No matter what we do, we can never prepare for all the variables that could undermine a project, initiative, or our personal performance over the next year. This is where the "pre-mortem" can come in handy.

While the post-mortem happens before a project to figure out what went wrong, a pre-mortem occurs before a project to try to predict what could go wrong and how to mitigate for those obstacles.

One use of a pre-mortem is for a team to gather and review an upcoming project as if it had already been completed but failed miserably. Each team member is asked privately create a list of what could have caused that failure. They then come together and share their lists. Working together, the group creates plans to prepare for, and thus avoid, those sources of failure or to modify the plan accordingly.

It is simple, as with the post-mortem, to use the pre-mortem as the basis for how you approach the upcoming year. Take these steps:

- List what you hope to achieve for the next year. Not just your official job objectives, but also your personal development goals.

- Look at each one and visualize yourself having failed to achieve them at the end of the year.

- List all the possible reasons for that failure.

- Break your list into four categories: 1. Things I did, 2. Things I didn't do, 3. Things others did, and 4. Things others didn't do.

- Plan to mitigate possible sources of failure.

Again, this is not rocket science. The trick is taking the time to do it. In this season of gift giving, give yourself a gift and take a little time out to do a post-mortem and a pre-mortem. It may be the best gift you get this year.

Leadership as a Liberal Art: A Reading List for Leaders

A theme pops up in coaching sessions with different clients. In separate meetings over the past week, three senior vice presidents raised the topic of books and what books, or kinds of books, leaders should read. One also asked, "In your experience, are most senior leaders voracious readers? I get different answers when I talk to people."

I thought about it for a moment, and responded that not every senior leader I knew was a voracious reader, but the most successful among them were voraciously curious and they sought to expand their understanding of the world whenever possible. A broad base of knowledge about the world simply equips you to be better armed to address the challenges that come your way.

Peter Drucker famously wrote that management "… deals with action and application; and its test is its results. This makes it a technology. But management also deals with people, their values, their growth and development—and this makes it a humanity…. Management is thus what tradition used to call a 'liberal art': 'liberal' because it deals with the fundamentals of knowledge, self-knowledge, wisdom, and leadership; 'art' because it is practice and application. Managers draw on all the knowledge and insights of the humanities and the social sciences—on psychology and philosophy, on economics and on history, on the physical sciences and on ethics." (*The New Realities*)

So, whether they know it or not, most leaders are students of the world, though the way they prepare for the pop quizzes–the countless tests and tribulations that arise to face a senior leader–may vary. For some, this preparation includes a lot of reading, for others it is traveling or talking to people. Still others prefer watching documentaries, or listening to audio courses or podcasts. People learn in different ways, so how you learn is not the point; that you learn is what matters.

Putting Together Your Curriculum

Everyone's interests and needs are different and a good liberal arts education is broad while allowing one to go deeper in areas of particular interest. In the rest of this post I will recommend some classics as well as some general overviews of a particular topic. The reader is encouraged to dive in deeper when curiosity strikes.

Leadership and Management

One of my clients was explaining how he used to read all the latest leadership books, but now he didn't find them very interesting. This was hardly surprising, I replied; as an SVP and functional head in a multibillion dollar business sector, you should find most of what appears in popular leadership self-help books to be a bit beneath you. The truth is, while many leadership books contain useful tips, most of them are not going to be of much value to senior leaders. One exception I would point out, is Drucker himself. Alfred North Whitehead is alleged to have said that all western philosophy is a series of footnotes to Plato. In the same way, just about any good idea found in most management books was already written by Drucker. Save yourself time and energy and go back and read Drucker when the desire to read a leadership book arises. *The Essential Drucker* and *The Effective Executive* are a great start. I also recommend the *US Army Leadership Handbook*, the best nuts-and-bolts leadership book you'll find.

Biography and History

Many leaders want to learn by example from great leaders, so they turn to biography when they become bored with leadership self-help books. Biographies of great leaders can be very informative, and authors such as Robert Caro, Jon Meacham, Ron Chernow, Edmund Morris, Doris

Kearns Goodwin, and David McCullough can weave riveting tales. The thing to remember about biographies of great leaders, however, is that what worked for them may not necessarily work for you. Sometimes leaders succeed despite themselves, and sometimes their success was situational. A case in point is Churchill, whose leadership style was masterful during wartime but less so during peace. That said, reading biographies can be very informative, and one quickly finds that there are very few novel situations; if you are facing a leadership challenge, there is a good chance that someone has faced it before and learning how they met the challenge can save you a lot of headache and heartache.

Even more useful than reading biographies of great leaders, perhaps, is reading history. History provides context, and any piece of data is more useful when we understand the context. Companies often worry about losing tribal knowledge and try to manage their workforce so that all the senior workers, who carry that knowledge, don't leave at the same time. Someone has to educate the newer people. Part of being a leader is understanding the external forces that shape, hinder, or help the business. Not understanding history is the same as losing tribal knowledge in a workforce—understanding the context enables one to address circumstances more effectively. My favorite brief history overview is E.H. Gombrich's *A Little History of the World.* I frequently encourage clients to pick an era and region that is of particular interest to them and dig in, and to find an author who holds their attention and read a few of his or her books. It is hard to go wrong with Barbara Tuchman, Theodore White, William Dalrymple, Peter Ackroyd, and Simon Schama.

The Hard Sciences

Most leaders seem more comfortable with the hard sciences than with the soft sciences. That said, rounding out one's scientific literacy is as useful as it is intellectually stimulating. Natalie Angier's *The Canon: A Whirligig Tour of the Beautiful Basics of Science* and Hazen and

Trefil's *Science Matters: Achieving Scientific Literacy* are my favorite primers. I recently began reading William Bynum's *A Little History of Science* and am enjoying it as well. I tend to be drawn to the biological sciences, and always recommend that any thinking person develop a better understanding of Darwin's theory of natural selection, widely considered by scientists to be the most important idea, ever. One of my favorite introductions is David Sloan Wilson's *Evolution for Everyone: How Darwin's Theory Can Change the Way We Think About Our Lives*.

When it comes to physics, it is hard to beat Richard Feynman. Try *The Character of Physical Law* as a starting point. I also enjoyed Feynman's essays on the nature of science, *The Meaning of It All*. And, while I've never been able to wrap my head around relativity, I've found Albert Einstein's *Ideas and Opinions* to be riveting. Einstein demonstrates that, despite the stereotype, brilliant people need not be socially inept or narrow in scope.

Philosophy

Though Feynman, in particular, would never admit it, these last two works are better thought of as philosophy than hard science, and I think philosophy is the discipline most neglected by leaders. It is philosophy that teaches us how to think about the facts we learn, how to test ideas, how to order knowledge. It is philosophy that teaches us how to think critically, and every great leader I have known is a rigorous critical-thinker. Nigel Wharburton's *A Little History of Philosophy* (see what Gombrich started...) is a great introduction, as is his podcast *Philosophy Bites*. Since our view of the world influences how we lead others in it, being conscious of one's philosophical assumptions is a critical rite of passage for leaders. Every leader should wrestle with the implications of Plato's *Republic*, for example, or Machiavelli's *The Prince*. (I recommend reading about *The Republic* before trying to tackle the original; and *Simon Blackburn* is a good start.) I also think a book like Jim Holt's *Why Does the World*

Exist: An Existential Detective Story forces us to think about questions and challenge our assumptions.

Finally, the philosopher who I think every thoughtful person should be acquainted with is David Hume. Few minds had the clarity of Hume or the impact on the modern sensibility that he did.
Again, *Blackburn* provides a good introduction.

Psychology

"Amateur psychologist" is one of the hats that every leader must wear. While familiarity with theorists such as Freud, Jung, Adler, et al is useful, I think that more recent developments in the cognitive sciences are more valuable for leaders. I recommend Kahneman's *Thinking Fast and Slow* and Tavris and Aronson's *Mistakes Were Made (but not by me)*.

Mythology, Religion, and the Classics

Once, over dinner in a small town outside of Frankfurt, a client recommended that on my next visit I stay at a place called Hotel Bacchus. I replied that I would; "After all, any hotel named after the god of wine and fertility must be a great place," I joked. My host was taken aback and laughed. "Sorry," he said, "I'm just shocked to meet an American who knows who Bacchus was." To be a truly educated person, one should have at least a passing familiarity with mythology, religion, and the classics. Most of our culture is based on mythological stories of the gods, sacred texts, and the writings of Shakespeare, Homer, Ovid, etc. Ignorance of these underpinnings of culture is akin to being color blind; we see, but we lose the subtleties and the richness. Start with Joseph Campbell's *Myths to Live By*. I also recommend Stephen Prothero's *Religious Literacy*. (I'll note, by the way, that while Hotel Bacchus was a very pleasant hotel, there was nothing particularly bacchanalian about it.)

Today's global economy requires that all senior leaders must be global in their outlook. There are many useful books available on understanding different cultures, but among my favorites are Trompenaars and Hampden-Turner's *Riding the Waves of Culture*, Hooker's *Working Across Cultures*, and Cabrera and Unruh's *Being Global*. I also recommend international news publications such as *The Financial Times*, *The Economist*, and *Foreign Policy*, all of which have excellent apps and online editions.

Being global also means that many senior leaders travel extensively. Most of these trips are short and there is little spare time. However, I think it is critically important to occasionally allow for time to visit the places we are flying in and out of. A liberal arts education is incomplete without the inclusion of culture and travel allows for exposure to experiences one cannot get in any other way. Learn a few words of the local language, eat the local foods, visit museums and places of worship. It is one thing to see the Mona Lisa in a book; it is wholly another to stand in front of her. One cannot be unchanged standing in Paris's Pantheon, wandering through Istanbul's Blue Mosque or Cairo's Sultan Hassan Mosque, basking in the radiant colors of the El Grecos in Madrid's Prado, or walking into Florence's Santa Croce Cathedral and seeing the sarcophaguses of Michelangelo, Machiavelli, Rossini, and Galileo.

Beyond Books

Of course, there are other ways to learn. Most senior leaders don't have the time to take classes, but downloadable lectures and audiobooks are easily available. I like *The Great Courses* and *Audible.com*, and the free podcasts available on iTunes are a treasure trove.

The joy of a liberal arts education is that it presents life as an endless buffet. This list of recommendations is short and as notable for what it doesn't include as for what it does (I can't help but notice that it is English language- and US-centric; *c'est la vie*). Half the fun is designing your own curriculum and I hope this helps you get started.

Are You a Leader for the Future?

Every generation tends to think it is living in a uniquely revolutionary time. This generation may actually be correct—the world seems to be changing exponentially and to degrees that have not been seen since the Industrial Revolution.

Joshua Cooper Ramo, author of "The Seventh Sense," makes a compelling case for this view. Ramo, co-CEO of Kissinger Associates (yes, as in Henry Kissinger…), describes how the leader of the future will need a "seventh sense," an ability to see patterns and connections that are driven by technology and globalization in ways never before imagined.

Likewise, Microsoft CEO Satya Nadella made some interesting comments about artificial intelligence (AI) and its effect on leaders and workforces at the recent Aspen Ideas Festival.

According to "Fortune" magazine editor Alan Murray, Nadella pointed out that AI will increasingly dominate our lives and create "massive" workforce displacement. Challenges that Microsoft and most other companies will have to grapple with, according to Nadella, are:

"How do we create AI to augment human capabilities and enhance the human experience? What are the things we need to do so that human welfare is front and center? And that means building in trust, transparency, the ability to take back control, and infusing technology with human values and empathy."

Nadella went on to say that the AI revolution will happen faster than previous industrial revolutions, calling for "reskilling on a constant basis."

In order to be successful in the future, people will need capabilities to do things that machines can't. Among the skills that workers of the future will need are "empathy, creativity, curiosity, and the ability of humans to be able to explore things which are non-linear." Educators will need to understand that "a more diverse set of subjects, beyond STEM, could become even more important."

So, what does all this mean for leaders of the future?

One scenario is admittedly bleak—those displaced are not re-placed, leading to fewer people being employed, rising populism and anti-globalism, and a more-challenging business climate (think Brexit on a global scale). Those in the leadership classes who believe they are not among those who will be displaced by machines need to remember that fewer employees require fewer leaders to lead them. Competition for leadership roles will become more-fierce, and you will need to be equipped for that competition.

The second scenario is that this revolution, like those of the past, will increase net prosperity and employment in the long run. But if Ramo and Nadelli are right, the skills required for success will be much more focused on what are traditionally considered "soft skills"—empathy, communication, creativity, etc.

Under either scenario, competencies that today may fall into the "nice-to-have" category will be necessities. The leader of the future will need:

• Self-awareness—the foundation of adaptability and the ability to learn new skills and competencies.

• An understanding of human nature—the foundation of empathy, communication, and conflict management.

- Exceptional critical thinking and decision-making skills—the foundation of the ability to see the real patterns and connections amidst an avalanche of data and complexity.

- Curiosity and a global mindset—the foundation of creativity and innovation.

- The ability to execute—the foundation of the ability to respond quickly to an ever-changing world and bring products to market faster than the competition.

Are you ready for what is coming?

Beware the Cement Shoes

By Mario Sikora

Having lunch with a client the other day, we were joking about our kids' taste in music, their "practically socialist" sense of values when it comes to information sharing, and their seeming addiction to technology. He pointed out his awareness of, and concern about, falling into the "curmudgeonly old dad" role—the guy who finds himself always talking about how much better things were in "my day."

We talked about how natural that process is and how it seems to happen to every generation, but also of the dangers it poses to senior people still in the workforce wanting to stay relevant to their organization. As a senior executive leading other senior executives and recognizing the unprecedented rate of technological change we face, this was not idle speculation for him.

"How does one stay, as a 50-year old, someone whose feet are not set in cement?" he asked.

It was a great question, and one that too few people ask.

While it's not often spoken about publicly, a leader's fifties become a challenging time—they have risen to a high position in the organization and are making a high salary. They are experienced, but may be growing out of touch with new ways of doing things—more likely resistors than early adopters. There are fewer opportunities above them due to the narrowing nature of the corporate pyramid. Hungry, talented young executives below them are looking for a way up the ladder and the older leader is seen as a roadblock. Even other senior leaders in positions of power start to see them as an obstacle in the leadership-succession pipeline—highly paid but stale employees blocking the way for younger, less-costly, and energetic high-potential leaders with fresh ideas.

At the same time, other pressures on the leader increase: A longer lifespan, combined with changing practices for financing retirement, mean that people are working longer. Technology is changing ever faster and the world is becoming more globalized and diverse, and a generation that came of age in a slower and more local world struggle to keep up. Society values the young, new, and fresh more than the experienced, seasoned, and mature.

Keeping up is more difficult for us as we get older—and more important than ever. In fact, continued learning in an effort to stay current should be considered part of one's job in the same way that an athlete considers training to be part of the competition.

In order to stay more relevant, every leader should develop a plan for continued learning and cultivating curiosity. While this post is focused on leaders in the later-stages of their career, these practices are good for all of us to practice; they will help you develop habits of mind that will serve you well now—before it's too late.

Start with a learning plan. The best leaders are intellectually curious— they want to know things just for the sake of knowing things. Curiosity and breadth of knowledge feed creativity and innovation, allowing leaders to see connections and relationships that others don't. The pressures and time demands of business make it difficult to apply this curiosity, however, and it helps to have a plan and become disciplined in feeding the intellect. Each quarter of the year, focus on learning about a new topic. For example, the first quarter (i.e., the first three months of the year) can be devoted to, say, learning more about artificial intelligence; Q2 can be devoted to Chinese culture and business practices; Q3 can be devoted to Middle Eastern history; etc. The topics don't matter so much as the fact that you are continuing to learn and creating diversity in your subjects. I'm not suggesting that you attempt to become an expert on any of these topics—just that you devote some amount of time to understanding the basics.

In addition to the learning plan, leaders should get into the habit of asking themselves a series of questions on a regular schedule.

Daily: "What did I learn today?"

New information about the world is revealed constantly. A day that goes by in which you didn't learn anything is a day you have fallen behind. If you can't think of anything you learned, pick up a book or go online and learn something before the day is over.

Weekly: "What was I wrong about this week?"

One of the most important qualities of a sharp and curious mind is to identify when we are wrong or when we made a mistake. Most of us hate to be wrong (I know I do), but each time we realize we were wrong about something we have become wiser. In fact, the best way to stay intellectually fresh and pliable is to vigorously work to spot errors in our thinking and correct them.

Weekly: "What was the most interesting conversation I had this week?"

Did you talk to your neighbor about her days in the Peace Corps? Listen to a podcast interview with a foreign policy expert? Talk with a customer about industry trends? Reflecting on interesting conversations and their implications helps spur creativity and broadens our insights.

Monthly: "Where did I go that I never went before?"

I can't count how many executives I have talked to who have been all over the world but have never seen any of it. This is understandable—leaders with global responsibilities are extremely busy and can't go sightseeing every time they have to visit a factory in Asia or meet with a customer in Europe. They tend to fly into a place, do their business, and fly home. But they can also approach the rest of their lives the same way; it is easy to fall into the habit of only going to the same old places in an effort to be more efficient. But if we never go new places, even if it is something as simple as a new restaurant or a park in our neighborhood, we limit our experiences and become stale.

Quarterly: "What did I used to believe that I don't believe any more?"

Questioning our guiding assumptions and beliefs on a regular basis is a key to avoiding becoming the old curmudgeon. I'll offer an example: I used to believe that becoming too fixated on their devices would erode my children's social skills so I decided that none of them should have a cell phone until they were 12. The reality is that cell phones are an integral part of children's lives at an even earlier age and now even my 10-year old has a cell phone. Rather than making them socially inept, my sons live in a hybrid reality—part virtual, part real. Yes, their devices seem to be an extension of their hands, but they also go to the playground and play sports with other kids and they can still sit down and have a focused conversation with adults when they need to. Rather than being socially stunted, my sons are far more informed and socially networked than I was at their age. Realizing this has made me acutely aware of how integral digital technology is to their generation and has made me think far more deeply about the future trends of my industry.

It is very tempting to become stuck in our ways, to resist change, to dismiss the new and strange. But we do so at our peril, and my client's metaphor of having one's feet stuck in cement is a good one. It may feel cool and pleasant while the cement is being poured around our feet, but donning a pair of cement shoes has never led to a good outcome for anyone.

Managing Your Time–Important but Not Urgent

The reality for most of us is that there is always more to do than we have time for. There are lots of time- or task-management systems to help us organize and prioritize, but rarely do they leave us feeling like we are on top of everything we need to be on top of.

I tend to be a time-management pessimist–I don't think any system truly works in the way that we hope it will or that–given today's environment of stimulation overload and global competition–we will ever feel that we can get everything done that we would like to.

That said, the most successful people tend to at least seem like they manage their time well, and it is something we can all get better at, even if it is a bit of a Sisyphean task.

So, what can we do to manage our time better? I recommend three things:

1. *Accept that you will never get everything done, that the best any of us can do is get the most important things done.* This is an attitude shift, but a liberating one. When you accept the fact that you can't get everything done, you relax and start focus on the most important things. Keep two to-do lists–a master list of things you have to do, but then pick the 3-5 most important and put them on a separate list. When they are done, throw that list away and pick 3-5 more from the master list. Everything on your list is equally important and urgent? Fine, pick 3-5 at random and do them first.

2. *Develop processes.* Automate as much as possible. Einstein famously owned multiple shirts, trousers and jackets of the same style so he didn't have to think about what to wear. I don't recommend that,

for sure, but anything we can do to reduce the things we have to think about gives us more time for important things. Get very, very good at developing people and delegating to them. Spend a few minutes each day reviewing what you spent your time on. Ask, "What did I do that I didn't need to?" "Did it need to be done?" "Who could/should have done it?" Did I mention the importance of developing people? I can't emphasize it enough. ***Strong subordinates are the mark of a leader who can get things done.***

3. *Devote time to what is important but not urgent.* Stephen Covey's time-management model is based on four boxes: 1) Important/Urgent, 2) Important/Not Urgent, 3) Not Important/Urgent, and 4) Not Important/Not Urgent. It is the second box that we tend to devote the least attention to and the one that has the biggest payoff in the long-run. Unfortunately, they are always things that can wait until tomorrow, so they do. They include developing subordinates (did I mention how important that is?), creating the processes in the paragraph above, taking time to reflect and think strategically, etc. The most-effective people carve out and ruthlessly protect "white-space time" on their calendar–uninterrupted time for reflection, prioritizing, and working on activities that are important but not urgent.

Leaders Provide Clarity

Leaders, of course, do many things and have many responsibilities. It would be hard to find one more universally important to successful leadership than providing clarity.

Business, and life in general, is complex. Clarity cuts through complexity and simplifies an organizations goals, strategy, and tasks. Lack of clarity results in a number of problems:

Delay and hesitation–when people don't know where to go they often don't go anywhere or they go the wrong way, losing valuable time.

- Misallocated resources–time, money, and labor are wasted on activities and initiatives that are not relevant to the mission.

- Employee dissatisfaction–confusion and lack of direction create an environment for uncertainty and anxiety to seep in.

Clarity reduces these problems.

Unfortunately, most leaders are not as clear as they think they are. It is human nature to equate "clarity" with "I know what I want." However, just because you know what you want doesn't mean that others know what you want. The test of communication lies in whether or not the other person got the message we wanted them to get, not whether we were eloquent or charismatic in our delivery of the message. Focusing on clarity of intent in our communication is a metaskill that is worth developing; in other words, in addition to being (at least moderately) articulate and engaging when we communicate, we should ensure that we are clear as well.

A client of mine recently provided me with a good model for providing clarity that he learned in law school.

"We were told that, when preparing a brief, we should answer these questions: 'What is the point? What is all the noise about? What do you want from me?'"

I amend this a little bit (always trying to add even more clarity, after all...) and I encourage leaders to ask the following questions about important communications:

1. What is the key point that people need to know, stated clearly, simply, and directly?

2. Why do they need to know this? (That is, why is it relevant to them?)

3. What, exactly, do I want them to do about it? By when? And, Who, exactly, is being held accountable for it?

So, in the interest of clarity:

- It is your job as a leader to provide clarity to those you lead.

- If you don't, you will waste time and resources, and create dissatisfaction in your employees.

- I would like you to ask (and answer) the three questions above each time you communicate to your team about important matters.

Developing Talent, Part 1

"Sometimes it just comes down to, 'Will this person embarrass me?'"

A client recently expressed the desire to develop the qualities that would help him grow from being the kind of leader who can run a $200m business to the kind of leader who can run a business of $1bn or more. I have some opinions on what those qualities are since I've worked with a number of leaders who made this kind of jump in scale—some successfully, some not—and other leaders who were never given the chance to try. Rather than rely on my own outsider view, however, I decided to ask a dozen or so leaders who have been successful in roles where they had P & L responsibility of $1bn or more what they think those qualities are. I also asked a few HR leaders who have supported general managers at this level.

I was surprised by their responses. Actually, not necessarily by the content of their responses, but by their responsiveness. I could tell that I hit on a question that these leaders were interested in. For such busy people, their answers, even when short, were thoughtful and precise. Their responses showed that this was the kind of question that these people spent a lot of time thinking about (which is probably one of the reasons why they are in the positions they are in...).

There were a number of themes in their responses, such as balancing strategic focus with execution discipline, the ability to manage complexity, and the ability to communicate a consistent and clear vision throughout the organization. But probably the quality that came through the most loud and clear was the ability to find, develop, and appropriately deploy talent at all levels of the organization, along with an ability and willingness to deal with under-performers and not let underperformance linger in their organization.

Dealing with talent clearly mattered to these people, and a number of them said that they spend up to half of their time on matters related to talent. Think about that for a moment—50% of their time...

Unfortunately, there is no secret formula for managing talent, but leaders should become as conscious and deliberate about talent as they can be. They should think about and create their own personal process, but be flexible in that process.

They should think about and develop philosophy or set of basic guidelines for finding talent, for developing the people that work for them, and for ensuring that people are deployed in the right roles. They should also develop a philosophy or set of guidelines for addressing performance issues and moving under-performers either into a role where they can be successful or move them out of the organization.

Rather than present a set of guidelines, I here propose some questions for leaders to consider while creating their own guidelines, separated into a few categories.

Finding Talent

- Am I consistently evaluating people I meet outside of the company and considering them as potential talent? (Good leaders are always foraging for talent.)

- Am I building a reputation as being the kind of leader that talented people want to work for?

- Where/how have I been successful in finding talent in the past? Am I over-relying on a particular talent pool (such as a former company)? Am I under-utilizing any of those pools?

- How strong is my HR organization in finding talent?

- Do we use the best recruiters we can find?

Developing Talent

- Do I give regular, in-the-moment, and specific feedback to people in a candid but constructive way?

- Have I identified top talent and given them the tools and opportunities to grow? Do I coach them and regularly ask about their career goals? Do I remain objective in my evaluations of them, or do I let my personal feelings or history with them get in the way?

- Do I solicit feedback from their key stakeholders on their performance in a transparent way?

- Am I demanding that my subordinates have the same focus on talent that I do and that a talent mindset is being cascaded down through the organization?

- Am I ensuring that those people who are solid talent (but perhaps not top-talent) are remaining engaged and challenged?

- Do I give feedback to my peers on the talent in their organizations in a fair and objective way? (Criticism—even when intended as constructive—of someone else's subordinates should only be offered when absolutely necessary or when solicited; positive feedback should be offered liberally.)

- Who are my potential successors? (One of the most important questions a leader can ask!) What is the timeline for their succession readiness? What gaps exist before they could succeed me? What am I doing to help them close those gaps? Do they need development in hard skills, soft skills, or simply more time in their role?

Deploying Talent

- Are my people in the right roles?

- Who can be given more challenges? Who should have their scope reduced, narrowed, or modified?

- Am I rotating people at the right cadence so they don't get bored but also don't feel overwhelmed?

- Who is a flight risk or recruitment risk? Do I need to keep them? How can I do so?

Addressing Non-performance

Dealing with non-performance is rarely a technical matter—any decent HR department can provide the necessary guidance on how to move someone out of their role or out of the company. Rather, it is usually an emotional matter—people either fear conflict or let sentiment get in the way—or they don't have a replacement ready. The points above should take care of the latter issue. When it comes to the emotional challenges, leaders should ask themselves:

- Is my avoidance of conflict making matters worse in the long run? How smart is that?

- Am I really doing this person a favor by letting this drag on?

- Am I alienating other subordinates by tolerating this situation?

- How am I jeopardizing my success and reputation, the success of the team, and the success of the company by allowing this to continue?

- How would I want to be treated in this situation?

Michael Mauboussin, whose books on decision-making are essential reading in my view, was asked in an interview about his general rules for decision making and if they could be shared a nutshell. His response was that if it is a linear problem, you should evaluate all the empirical evidence as clearly and thoroughly as you can and then do what the evidence suggests. If it is a non-linear problem, you should evaluate the evidence as clearly and thoroughly as you can, and then go with your gut. His point is that some problems don't have simple and clear solutions, and when faced with these situations, *not* deciding does not make things any better.

This brings us back to the question with which I started this interview. There are few challenges more non-linear than assessing talent. While I highly encourage leaders to establish guiding principles regarding talent, these guidelines are rarely completely sufficient (especially when it comes to hiring or promoting people). At some point, you just have to do as much due diligence as you can and then trust your gut. But it helps to know what your "gut-check" question is.

The gut-check question I cited at the outset—"Will this person embarrass me?" was shared by the president of a $3.5 bn segment in a telecom company, and it was as good as any I've heard. Your gut-check question may be different, but you should know what it is. Without it, leaders end up avoiding talent decisions in the quest for more information that will end up being meaningless anyway. Your gut-check question allows you to be decisive, another necessary quality that allows leaders to scale.

Developing Talent, Part 2

My last article talked about the importance of finding, developing, and deploying talent to a leader's ability to "scale"—to take on larger roles and responsibilities. The article was a high-level overview, more focused on a leader's talent philosophy than on the "what to do" of talent development.

Over lunch last week, a client asked if I had a template for developing people. While I think that each leader does well to develop his or her own template, I'll offer some thoughts to get you started.

Assessment

Developing talent starts with the assessment of the individual against the requirements of the role they currently have and against the requirements for possible future roles. While there are many ways to do this, here is one I recommend to my clients as a starting point:

- A1 = Employee exceeds the requirements of the current role and is ready for advancement now.

- A2 = Employee exceeds the requirements of the role but still needs some development to be ready for advancement.

- B1 = Employee meets the requirements of the role and has the potential to take on more responsibility; he or she can become an A employee with further development.

- B2 = Employee meets the requirements of the current role but will probably not advance further.

- C1 = Employee does not meet the requirements of the current role but can become a B employee with additional development.

- C2 = Employee does not meet the requirements of the current role and does not seem to have the willingness or capacity to meet those expectations.

This "A," "B," and "C" terminology may seem a little outdated—a hold-over from the day's when Jack Welch's "rank and yank" model was popular—and some people prefer using more-euphemistic terms such as "top talent." The point is not the terminology, but that you have some mental model that works for you in assessing people. A model like this is something to guide your thinking, not to use to publicly label other people.

Development

I generally encourage leaders to focus on C2 and A2 employees first (for reasons that will become clear), but let's look at all six categories in turn starting with the last.

What to do with C2 Employees

I generally encourage my clients to focus on C2 employees first. Employees who are underperforming and not showing the willingness or capacity to meet the requirements of their role are a significant drain on the organization. They leave gaps that others need to step in and fill, they make other employees resentful, they take up far too much of the leader's time and energy, and their continued presence undermines the leader's credibility regarding their commitment to success and ability to address challenging situations. They must be dealt with fairly and objectively, but also without undue hesitation.

A leader needs to exercise due diligence and assess whether the C2 employee can become a B employee (or better) in a different role within the team or elsewhere in the company, or if there is simply not a role in the company that fits the capabilities or aspirations of the employee. In the former situation, the leader should work to quickly reassign the employee; in the latter situation the leader should work with Human Resources to start moving the individual out of the company.*

What to do with C1 Employees

Many large companies have thorough and detailed yearly review processes. These processes usually set goals for the employee and have some system of tracking the employee's progress toward those goals. As long as they are taken seriously and not too onerous, such processes are very useful. I recommend something a little different, however, either in place of or in addition to such processes—a simple three-column employee development plan.

- Column 1—What is this person's strengths and what can I do to help them utilize those strengths more?

- Column 2—What improvements need to be made to get this person from where they are today to performing at the level I expect?

- Column 3—What am *I* going to do to help this person make this progress? What is my timeline for doing so? How will I measure success?

This third column is the important distinction—it is making a commitment to help the employee improve, and actively engaging in that improvement, rather than simply placing the expectation on them to figure out how to grow. Yes, this requires more time and energy from the leader, but as we saw in the last article—talent development is one of the most important parts of a leader's job and if you don't spend time and energy on it you will eventually fail.

What to do with B2 Employees

There is nothing inherently wrong with being a B2 employee or having some of them on the team. Most people reach a point where they are content with their circumstances and do not wish to take on further challenges. Many people choose the satisfaction of an interesting-but-not-overly demanding job and the ability to have more time in their home life. Or, they may recognize their natural limitations and not want to over-reach and fail. Most teams have roles that are well-suited for such people—people who are steady, dependable, and competent. As long as they are not holding the team back and they stay current on the skills necessary for the role—that is, as long as they don't become C employees—I encourage leaders to leave well-enough alone. Monitor these individuals and ensure that they keep current, make sure that they stay motivated, but don't invest extra time and energy on their development.

What to do with B1 Employees

B1 employees provide an opportunity to improve the team. The goal of a leader when it comes to developing talent is to keep anyone who *can* grow on a path of growth. Continuous improvement is the lifeblood of an organization and only occurs if the individuals who make up the organization keep improving (with the B2 exceptions noted previously). If a leader has B1 employees—people who meet expectations and have potential to take on more with some development—I suggest that they implement the three-column development plan mentioned above, *but not until they have addressed their A2 employees.*

What to do with A2 Employees

The leader should spend most of their time and energy on A2 employees—those who exceed expectations but are not quite ready for advancement yet.

While it is nice to think that we are all equal in potential, we are not. Some people have a unique combination of drive, natural talent, and acquired skills that make them better-suited for certain activities than other people. I can shoot a basketball, but I am not Stephan Curry and no amount of work will make me Stephan Curry.** A1 and A2 employees have a disproportionate influence on the team's performance and any investment of time and energy in their development is rewarded exponentially. After addressing C2 employee situations, the smart thing for leaders to do is focus on the development of A2 employees.

If you have A2 employees, use the three-column plan, but do so with more detail. Be clear with the employee that you are investing in their development and see opportunity for advancement or expanded responsibility for them with the proper growth (but never make promises to the employee you may not be able to keep!). Be very specific about the skills gap between where they are now and where they could be. Be sure to give positive feedback whenever possible (we all like encouragement from the boss; high-achievers need it like oxygen), and never miss an opportunity to give constructive feedback. Always frame the constructive feedback as a way of preparing for something bigger and better in the future to ensure the employee maintains their confidence.

What to do with A1 Employees

There is a scene in the movie "Full Metal Jacket" where, after a torturous 8 weeks of basic training, the Marine drill instructors are starting to lose control of the recruits. The recruits are ready for more, and they are chomping at the bit to go to war. A1 employees—those who exceed expectations and are ready for advancement—are like those Marine recruits. They need to be challenged and stretched or else they will rebel or move to another company.

It is vital that a leader not become complacent with such employees and assume that they will continue happily in their current role. You must keep them busy and look for opportunities for them within the company. You must also make sure that you have identified and groomed their successor, because A1 employees leave a company in which they do not see further opportunity to grow and you don't want to be caught with a big hole in your team.

Special cases—B1 Employees in A Roles

One of the more challenging situations leaders face is when they have a B1 employee in a role for which they need an A employee. Yes, the B employee is meeting the current expectations, but due to market dynamics, company reorganization, or other factors the demands of the role are changing and more is needed for the team to be successful. It is also possible that a leader can have an A2 employee in a role but due to changing demands of the role the employee becomes a B1 employee.

In either situation, it is important for the leader to act. Be very candid with the employee about the situation. Explain that it is related to changing circumstances rather than the fault of the individual per se. But also be clear that it requires the employee to strive to improve. In such situations, it is incumbent upon the leader to actively engage in the development of the employee, but also be realistic about whether the individual can meet the demands of the new situation.

It is important for the leader in this situation to:

- Clearly describe the situation and changing expectations, while acknowledging the past accomplishments of the individual.

- Clearly identify the areas that require improvement and set specific metrics and deadlines for progress. A leader cannot spend too much time clearly articulating their expectations—

what needs to change, why it needs to change, and by when it needs to change should be spelled out in writing.

- Help the person when you are able do so personally, but don't hesitate to get them specific skill training or executive coaching. A leader owes such investment to someone who has contributed to the company and is working in good faith to improve performance so they can continue to contribute.

- Do not unnecessarily delay decisions to make personnel changes while still ensuring that you treat people fairly. It is morally, ethically, and legally appropriate, but it also influences the way your other employees view you. If they see you treating someone unfairly, they will expect the same treatment. And nothing saps motivation more quickly than an employee's concern that they will not be treated fairly. If a B1 employee is not making it in an A role, move them gently but move them nonetheless.

Most of what is written here applies to developing a leader's direct reports. Most senior leaders also have layers of indirect reports—people who report to people who report to them—and the leader should take responsibility for ensuring leadership development at all levels of the organization. Not only should they take the actions described here, they should insist that their subordinates take these actions with *their* subordinates. Leaders should take every opportunity to observe and assess employees multiple levels below them. They should not only hold their subordinates accountable for employee development, they should challenge their direct team members on their assessments and plans for development.

Leaders should always remember that they are ultimately responsible for talent from the bottom of their organization to the top. If your direct reports are not developing *their* direct reports, it is *your* fault.

The advice shared here is only a starting point—talent development is a broad topic and leaders should immerse themselves in it. Treat it as a skill you should study until the end of your career. Below are a few good books to get you started.

Books on Talent Development:

- *Topgrading* by Bradfort D. Smart

- *For Your Improvement: A Development and Coaching Guide* by Michael M. Lombardo and Robert W. Eichinger

- *Leaders at All Levels* by Ram Charan

- *Superbosses: How Exceptional Leaders Master the Flow of Talent* by Sydney Finkelstein

- *The Leadership Pipeline* by Ram Charan, Stephen Drotter, and James Noel

*It is relatively easy to move people out of the company (a euphemism for "fire the person") in the US, but this is not the case in many countries. In countries with more challenging labor laws the leader must get more creative, but that is beyond the scope of this article.

**For my non-US friends, Curry is one of the most gifted basketball players in the game.

Making Friends (and Doing Business) Around the World: Three Simple Things to Do on Your Next Trip
As the saying goes, when in Rome...

I recently learned to tango.

Well, let's say I learned eight or ten tango steps.

Well, to be completely honest, despite being (officially) the world's most awkward dancer, I should say that I recently joined my hosts and fellow conference attendees for a tango lesson at party in Buenos Aires. I did so because, despite my almost-paralyzing self-consciousness and the humiliation that was sure to follow, I was not going to let down my hosts by not taking part in an activity that was important to them.

Yes, my dancing was awkward and humiliating and I've had to bribe friends to keep the videos off social media. But by participating in the tango lessons I made much deeper bonds with people I barely knew than I could have any other way.

Many of my clients are executives in multinational organizations who spend as much time traveling--often internationally--as they do at the home office. Their trips often involve meetings with customers and employees from the countries they are visiting, but rarely do they have time to get out and visit the region they are in. This is understandable-- they are on business trips, not vacations. But I am frequently surprised when I learn that my clients travel to exotic places but stay in US hotel chains, eat the same foods they would at home, and learn nothing about the place they are in (yes, people from the US seem most guilty of this).

They don't seem to realize that they are missing opportunities for business growth and personal enrichment when they travel in a bubble.

I have the good fortune to get paid to travel to a lot of interesting places and meet interesting people, and I have come to realize that there are a few simple things you can do to quickly build deeper bonds with people in other countries that will help you make friends and build your business.

1. Sample the local foods.

People in most countries are proud of their local cuisine. I know that I can't wait to take people who visit me to Geno's for a cheesesteak in the heart of South Philly, and most people are similarly eager to see the look on your face when you bite into a regional delicacy. Over the years, I have been surprised by how delighted people are when I sample anything that comes my way. One of the reasons for that delight is that a surprising number of people won't eat their foods. The same rule applies to cultural traditions: In Colombia? Dance salsa if asked. In Portugal? Listen to Fado. In Hong Kong? Don't ask for a fork.

2. Learn a few simple words in the local language.

My father spoke four languages and I am always embarrassed that I only speak one. But wherever I go I try to learn just a few words--thank you, please, hello, the local toast, etc., and I'm always impressed at the response people have when I use them--no matter how awkward my pronunciation. Thanking a taxi driver in Cairo with a simple "a shukraan" or greeting your audience in Korea with "annyeong haseyo" is a very simple way to build good will. Ten minutes with Google Translate before a trip is one of the best investments of time you can make.

On the issue of language, it is common for people outside the US who speak even relatively good English to be embarrassed about their English fluency. Always take the opportunity to tell them how impressed you are with their ability, and be sure to point out how much better they speak your language then you speak theirs.

One other semi-related issue: If you are from the US, refrain from calling yourself an "American." It is a common usage--especially in

Europe--but it can easily offend people from the rest of the Americas, from Canada down to Patagonia. It may be awkward to refer to your self as "from the US" but it will impress the culturally asture and eliminate one possibility of offending others.

3. Seek to learn, not to teach.

Granted, most of my trips outside the US are to teach something to someone, but when I am not working I stop teaching and start asking questions. When I am in a different country I want to know about the place, the people, the culture. I will tell people about life in the US if they really, really want to know, but given the US's dominance in world media, people have a general idea of what life is like in the place I live. People love to talk about themselves and their life--give them the chance to do so and educate yourself in the process. There is no better way to learn about a place than through the eyes of the people who live there; asking people questions--and genuinely listening to the answers--is one of the quickest ways to enrich both your relationships and your life.

Non-Transactional Networking

When I joined the ranks of the self-employed many years ago, I did what all the books tell you to do: Get out and meet people–join the chamber of commerce and relevant professional associations. I attended networking events in these groups and hated every minute of it. They were hotbeds of the worst kind of *transactional* networking, which I think of as an encounter focused on an immediate quid pro quo.

As I think back on those events, it seems like the evening consisted mainly of people approaching me with the goal to sell me insurance or financial services while I clocked how quickly they disengaged upon finding out that I was not a buyer. The irony is that had any of those young, hungry sales reps taken a few minutes to show interest in me, I may have been much more inclined to keep their business card and refer potential buyers to them. Because they were focused on transacting with me, then and there, they missed the possibility of tapping into my network over the long term.

This is what most people think of when they think of "networking"— entering into a thinly veiled marketplace with aggressive hawkers selling trinkets. No one wants to be seen as such a hawker, and no one wants to be hawked at, and many people use this as a rationale for not networking at all.

Granted, there is a time and place for transactional networking–after all, when you want to buy something, you go to the market. But, you see very few senior leaders at such events–they tend to have developed better methods.

Non-Transactional Networking

An alternative approach is what I call "non-transactional networking." It is, admittedly, a bit of a misnomer, but it conveys a fundamental message–while we need to be smart and deliberate about our networking, we never know where a useful connection will come from or what seed, once planted, will ultimately bear fruit. Thus, the non-transactional networker understands that the best way to build relationships is to have a seemingly contradictory approach– understanding that not every seed will bear fruit but also that you will end up with more fruit if you plant more seeds and gently nurture them. Non-transactional networkers do hope for a transaction–they would like to eventually receive some benefit from their engagements, but they are willing to engage with an attitude that they won't gain anything from the initial encounter and may not ever receive anything, but one never knows...

Non-transactional networkers also know that jumping right to the task at hand and dominating the conversation rather than allowing others to share their ideas will cause you to miss out on what can be very useful information. You rarely learn anything by talking...

Sticking with our seed metaphor, I am not suggesting that you throw seeds carelessly on rock or sand, chatting up everyone you encounter. Rather, you should understand where the seeds might grow and then plant liberally. Non-transactional networking relies on balancing effectiveness with non-attachment to the results. I'm also not suggesting that you stand mutely while someone bores you with endless tales of uninteresting things; it is essential to learn the art of the skillful exit.

The irony is that this non-transactional attitude takes much of the stress out of networking–it means that instead of feeling like you have wasted your time if you didn't "close" during the interaction, you can just relax and enjoy talking to people with the understanding that the more people you know–and who know you–the more likely some opportunity or advantage will occur from places you could have never predicted.

"Lincoln," and the Politics of Organizations

The movie "Lincoln" is a two-and-a-half-hour master course in politics. Focusing on Lincoln's efforts to pass the 13th amendment to end slavery and featuring a spellbinding performance by Daniel Day-Lewis and a brilliant script by Tony Kushner, the movie should be mandatory viewing for leaders of all types. It makes crystal clear why "politics" and leadership are intricately and inseparably linked.

It's common for my coaching clients to sneer at the mere mention of the words "office politics." Most people are uncomfortable with the idea that simply working hard and doing what is right is not all that matters in our work life, that we sometimes have to "play the game" in order to see our goals come to fruition.

I have seen two major reasons for the disdain of organizational politics:

First, we have all seen people who seem to use political skills untethered by ethics. That is, they use deception, cronyism, backstabbing, and intimidation to get their personal goals. They advance their agenda independent of the good of others, and they seem to lack substance. No one wants to be *that* person so we express disdain for office politics and avoid them.

Second, organizational politics can be difficult and require skills that we don't learn in a classroom. Those who disdain organizational politics usually don't want to face this fact--that they don't have good political skills and it would take work to develop them--preferring to simply demonize the activity rather than try to learn how to do it effectively.

The first objection is a straw-man argument, however--focusing on gross generalizations that are often not true of effective office politicians. Yes, some people are Machiavellian, self-serving, substance-free incompetents who get ahead because of their ability to schmooze; but the number of these people is smaller than we might suspect. Some people are effective politicians and do so to further an agenda of substance and benefit for the group. "Lincoln" dismisses this objection when Lincoln says to Rep. Thaddeus Stevens, a staunch anti-slavery advocate, "What good does it have true north if you get lost in the swamps on your way there?"

The second objection is usually the true obstacle, even if we are not conscious of how it shapes our resistance. Simply put, organizational politicking is hard work (another point that "Lincoln" demonstrates).

One definition of "politics" from Merriam-Webster Online is *the total complex of relations between people living in society*. Think about that for a moment--"the total complex of relations...." People are complicated and often contradictory. They often don't know what they really want, and when they do they don't always know the best way to get it so they often flounder around relying on emotion and gut intuitions rather than clear logic and rationality.

Interacting with one person is challenging enough; when you start adding multiple stakeholders with multiple agendas, the *complex of relations* can become daunting. The more important the goal, the more treacherous and challenging the waters become. It is tempting to throw up our hands and reject the politics of getting things done as an ignoble undertaking.

But rejecting the politics of getting things done means that we never reach true north; we get lost in the swamps. Thus, those who want to really get things done, who want to accomplish big things, who want to see their good ideas come to fruition, must "go back to school" and learn those abilities that you didn't learn earlier.* Those abilities include developing general qualities such as emotional intelligence, strategic skills such as an understanding of power dynamics and basic psychology, and tactical skills such as the ability to compromise and find a quid pro quo.

Chris Argyris's idea of "skilled incompetence" is important here, the idea that the more successful (or perhaps just the older) one becomes the more psychologically difficult it is to place oneself in the beginner's role and learn the basics of a given task or competence.

Increasing Political Savvy

I wrote about the movie "Lincoln" and its depiction of politics in action in my last article. Now, we'll take a look at some of the things you can do to increase your political savvy and thereby increase your ability to be effective and exercise influence.

Most of us have a complicated relationship with what is generally referred to as "political savvy" in organizations, and our view of the term is generally negative. We all know someone who rose to a position of power and influence based on political skills, self-promotion, and connections rather than merit. None of us want to be *that* person. Unfortunately, in our efforts not to be that person we overreact and develop an aversion to politics that can undermine our ability to influence others.

This phenomenon is one of the most common obstacles leaders face when trying to move from middle management to senior management: they have allowed their aversion to being *that person* undermine the development of their influencing skills. As a result of actively avoiding politics, they lack political savvy.

Here are some ways to improve this important competence.

The first thing someone has to do in becoming political savvy is to realize the value of it and be very clear about why developing more of it is in your best interests. As "Lincoln" demonstrates, we can achieve noble ends with politics as well as nefarious ends, and it does little good to "have a True North if we get lost in the swamps on the way there." Good leaders commit to developing good political skills with the understanding that they are necessary to getting good work done.

A second objection is that organizational politics waste time that could be spent *working*. I italicize *working* in this instance because organizational politics are also hard work! And they are a *necessary* part of work. Whenever two or more people are affected by an action, conflicting needs and values come into play. The way we resolve these conflicts is through *politics*. Ignoring those needs and value conflicts will ensure that our initiatives stall. Politics are part of the task, not a needless distraction from work.

So, once we're committed to becoming more politically savvy, what can we do?

- *It always helps to start with a best practice analysis, and the best people to analyze are those around you who are politically savvy.* Look for those who influence others in a way that you respect rather than focusing on those who do it in a superficial or substance-less style. Make a list of the things they do–how they address people, how they speak, how they listen, how they get things done. Pick two or three things from that list that you would feel comfortable doing and then create an action plan to start doing them.

- *Become a student of politics, influence, and power.* Read books on leaders and pay attention how they exercise politics. Be very careful here: Some will read a biography of a famous leader such as, say, Patton and think that his style–tough, demanding, abrasive–is the best way to lead. In fact, it was Patton's lack of political savvy that ultimately hindered him from achieving even more than he did. Learn to distinguish between the political capabilities that result in a leader's success and the incidental qualities that may have held them back.

- *Network, network, network.* Stretch outside your normal circle and get to know people. Identify influencers in your organization and find a way to interact with them. Be strategic about networking with influencers and don't waste their time. Find a way that you can be helpful to them. It is also very effective to ask them for a small favor. We all tend to raise the value of those in whom we invest in some way (psychologists call this "an investment bias"); if you can get an influencer to do you a small favor that doesn't cost them much time or energy, they will naturally see you as more valuable and worth-knowing than they did before.

• *Focus on feelings*. Like it are not, we are emotion-driven creatures rather than data-driven creatures. We feel first; second, we try to figure out why we feel a certain way or simply rationalize our emotion-driven decisions. Of course, we always want to try to overcome this pattern in ourselves and be as data-driven as possible, but we have to understand that if we want to influence people we have to speak to their emotions and support it with data. Good politicians know that you campaign in poetry and you govern in prose. Effective "campaigning" for your ideas is part of being an influencer, and this is done through an acknowledgement of and appeal to the emotions of others (the poetry). Of course, the campaigning must be followed up with data, strategy, and execution (the prose). A simple exercise when trying to influence others is to give some thought to how you want people to *feel about themselves* (rather than about *you*), and tailor your message accordingly.

Politics can be treacherous, and many people do unsavory and self-serving things through political means. However, being politically savvy is the only way to get things done. As the movie Lincoln said, you can only get to the goal if you don't get lost in the swamps along the way.

Becoming A Skillful Navigator

Rob is a brilliant, charismatic engineering sales and marketing leader for a mid-sized manufacturing company. He is in his mid-forties and already been successful in a number of smaller companies, and his new company was excited to bring him onto the team two years ago.

During the interview process, Rob wowed the leadership team with his ideas on how he could take the organization in a whole new direction with their digital sales support systems. However, before long his ideas got bogged down in the efforts to implement them. Key stakeholders in the business verticals started to complain that Rob's ideas were not practical for their kind of products or market. They said that when they tried to explain the "realities" to him it was difficult to get him to listen, and his follow-up actions after those meetings did not take their feedback into account.

However, no one directly brought the complaints to Rob's attention and he thought everything was fine. As I spoke to others in the company it was clear that this was becoming Rob's reputation—big-but-impractical ideas out of touch with the realities of this particular company, and an unwillingness or inability to listen. Others, including his boss, expected him to read between the lines and figure out the problem, but he was missing all the signals and he was losing credibility without knowing it.

****

Rob's story is not uncommon. Recently, I've had a number of clients who have been very successful over the course of their careers but have recently gotten side-tracked due to one issue—having blind spots about their inability to read the shifting political culture in their organizations and react to them accordingly.

This article is about how to fix that and how to become more attuned to the subtlety of social and political dynamics in organizations (or any group). I want to frame it through the lens of the three instinctual domains—Preserving, Navigating, and Transmitting.

While I've written about these three instinctual domains and our tendency to non-consciously focus on, or be biased toward, one of them in other articles. Here is a very brief description of each:

The *Preserving* domain is a group of instinctual impulses that relates to nesting and nurturing needs. They are inclinations to ensure we have the resources we need to survive, to ensure that we are safe and secure, to ensure shelter and comfort. In addition to these fundamental "self"-preservation needs, however, this domain also includes preservation of artifacts, traditions, our offspring, and those people we hold dear. It is an innate desire to ensure not only that we survive, but that those who carry our genes survive and prosper, and that we have the resources necessary to ensure that survival.

The instinctual drives in the *Navigating* domain help us navigate or orient to the group. They help us understand group dynamics, social status, and cultural mores and they equip us with skills that enable us to know who we can trust and develop reciprocal relationships with. As social creatures, we need to understand how the group works and how to be accepted into it. We have to gather information about others but only reveal enough about ourselves to maintain a favorable reputation. We need to know who is in "the tribe" and who is not, and how we can ensure we remain a part of the social security network. The navigating behaviors help us do that.

The Transmitting domain of instinctual drives increases the likelihood that we will attract the attention of others and it equips us to demonstrate the value of our ideas, values, creations, or genes. This domain is about attention and intensity; it is about display and enticement. Commonly thought of as being focused on one-to-one relationships, it is more accurate to say that this group of instinctual behaviors enhances our ability to make sure some part of ourselves passes on to the next generation.

Rob's instinctual bias is toward the Transmitting domain, and despite all of their many talents, people with this bias often lack the ability to skillfully Navigate their social environment. They are charming and apparently extroverted, they can entrance people with a good story and are often surrounded by attentive people, but this ability to engage an audience is not the same thing as being able to read the subtle cues coming back from others or the implicit currents that often shape a group.

Those with a transmitter instinctual bias may seem very social in a given environment, but they are usually not effective Navigators.

Of course, all of us, no matter what our instinctual bias, could become more skillful in our navigating, and how to do that is what we will focus on here.

To become a good Navigator, we need to start with understanding a couple of basic realities:

- All humans have evolved mental adaptations that help them both compete and cooperate with others, and we are often both competing and cooperating with the same people at the same time. (An example is coworkers on a project team who need to collaborate to get the project done but are also competing for the next promotion that becomes available.)

- Many of these mechanisms help us track who we can reciprocate with and who we can trust. They do this through attunement to subtle behaviors among people, and they involve

190

watching, listening, and evaluating. They involve sharing information as well, but in a controlled and managed way.

- Further, it is the Navigating skills that allow us to, well, navigate through the complex realities of being part of a social species. Everyone we meet is seeking to satisfy their own needs, to be happy, to be successful. In any group, it is likely that the needs of some will conflict with the needs of others. Being able to effectively manage competing needs is dependent on the navigating domain of instinctual behaviors.

There are ways to Navigate that are "good" and ways that are "bad." In fact, we can put those behaviors into three categories:

- *Harmful Navigating* is when we use navigating behaviors to advance our interests at the expense of others or over-emphasize navigating behaviors to our own detriment because we fail to attend to other instinctual needs.

- *Non-transactional Navigating* is the instinctual behaviors that those with a navigating instinctual bias generally do well and without thinking. They are the seemingly innocuous interactions we have with people during which the Navigator shares information but more so seeks information that may not have an immediate benefit but could be useful someday.

- *Skillful Navigating* is when we use our political skills to effectively further our agenda or interests in a way that, at best, also furthers the agendas of others or, at worst, does no harm to others.

The path to becoming an effective Navigator is to minimize harmful navigating, increase the amount and deliberateness of the non-transactional navigating you do, and become more effective at skillful navigating.

Skillful Navigating is very similar to "political savvy," though it is a much-less loaded term and, I believe, has broader implications. For some, the idea of becoming a more skillful navigator brings up fears of showing a lack of integrity similar to what they have perceived in people who they consider to be overly "political." This is a valid concern, but it is important to remember that it is not a binary choice—you can be both a skillful navigator and have high integrity. There is a great scene in the movie "Lincoln" when one of Lincoln's advisors is frustrated at his willingness to compromise, cajole, and collaborate with unlikeable people. Lincoln's response is "What good is it to have a true north if you get lost in the swamp on your way there?" This is probably a fictional conversation, but it illustrates that Lincoln knew that both integrity *and* political skill were needed to truly make things happen.

That said, there are some behaviors in this domain that fall into the "Harmful Navigating" category that we really should avoid, including:

- *Don't spread negative or hurtful gossip about others.* This will always come back to haunt you.

- *Don't start misleading gossip or share sensitive information.* Information is the coin of the realm in the Navigating domain; treat it appropriately and respectfully.

- *Don't focus only on your agenda.* Navigating is done best when we think "win-win" and help others accomplish their agenda while we accomplish ours.

- *Don't do all the talking.* Navigating involves sharing some information about yourself to build rapport, but is done best when you focus on inquiry, listening, and paying attention to the other person.

- *Don't be too clever.* Group dynamics are extremely complex and that complexity is easy to underestimate. Some, when attempting to be politically savvy, try to be too clever.

They think they can keep track of all the needs and goals of others, know all of the interrelationships of the people involved, and pull the right strings to get what they want. This is rarely the case—if we try to be too clever and too manipulative we will usually miss something important and our efforts will backfire. Candor and honesty combined with humility and sensitivity to relevant interests is most effective.

There can also be some downsides when people Navigate in ways that are not necessarily harmful but are not necessarily skillful. For example:

- They can be too consensus-oriented, overly fearful of offending others.

- They may be vague and non-committal, never fully revealing their point of view.

- They can resist making decisions until they feel that they have considered all the variables, and there are often a lot of variables.

- They can seem "two-faced," telling this person one thing and that person something else. This is often an issue of nuance and variance in what the navigator focuses on in each conversation rather than outright deception.

Non-transactional Navigating

The value of the instinctual Navigating adaptations is easy to underestimate because they don't typically have an immediate payoff, or a benefit that can be linearly identified. "Non-transactional" is a bit of a misnomer in that we hope to get some benefit from the interactions, even if we don't yet know what that benefit is or when we will receive it.

Non-transactional Navigating is like constantly planting seeds and nurturing those seeds when you know that only a fraction of the seeds will ultimately bear fruit, and you never really know which seeds are part of that fraction.

Here are some things to do to increase your effectiveness at non-transactional navigating.

- *Remember* that the core "purpose" of the Navigating instinctual bias is to collect information that can be useful some day and fit that information into organizing frameworks. Those frameworks can be loose and intuitive or they can be formal and structured.

- *Take any opportunity you can to meet new people.*

- *Make small talk* with people you wouldn't normally engage with, but do it in a way so that they are the focus of the conversation, not you.

- *Keep notes.* When you meet someone new, makes notes afterward of personal details you discovered—their interests, spouse's name and profession, etc. This will help you remember those details or serve as a reminder for you the next time you see them. People like to know you paid attention to them and remember them. Referring back to small details about the person goes a long way in building rapport.

- *Recognize the value of gossip,* but steer it toward positive areas when possible. Gossip serves to provide us information related to trust and reciprocity. It is also a mechanism to keep people in line with the group mores—our implicit fear of being gossiped about makes us think twice about crossing a line. Don't expect that it will ever go away—it won't.

- *Know who the connectors and influencers are.* There is something in anthropology referred to "Dunbar's Number." It is based on the premise that our brains have evolved to keep track of about 150 personal relationships. Some people seem to have a knack for either having a greater capacity than that or for maintaining relationships with well-connected and influential people. Maintaining relationships with such people increases your Dunbar number. The more people we have relationships with, directly or indirectly, the more effective and influential we can be.

- *Become a student of human nature.* Pay attention to what makes people tick, develop at least a passing knowledge of psychology.

- *Have a 'soft' networking plan.* Be deliberate in getting out and connecting with old friends and associates and cultivating new ones. Set a realistic weekly target and hold yourself accountable to it. Don't expect anything specific from these interactions. Just make it a habit and see what comes from it over the long term.

Skillful Navigating

Skillful Navigating is the art of not only surviving your social environment, but thriving in that environment in an appropriate and ethical way. The more complex an environment is, the more people and competing needs it includes, the more skillful we need to be.

Here are some things to work on to become a more-skillful navigator. It would be overwhelming to try to work on all of them at once, but you can pick one or two at a time that you think would be most beneficial.

Know your mission and be clear about it.

Spell out your mission or vision, your values, and your goals; put them into a concise elevator speech, and repeat it as often as possible. Make your vision compelling and help people see how it benefits them as well. Simplicity, clarity, and mutual benefit should be at the heart of any messages used during navigating efforts.

At first glance, this may seem to be more related to the Transmitting domain, but as we shall see a big part of skillful navigator is managing the perception others have of you. In any sort of leadership role, your mission is part of what you become identified with. Ensuring that you have clearly defined your mission helps you shape the narrative that becomes attached to you.

Know your desired audience and how they fit into the social terrain you face.

Be very specific about who the relevant stakeholders are (your audience) so you can tailor your communication accordingly. You need to know what the people you are trying to influence need/want so you can help them accomplish it on the way to accomplishing your mission.

Understand how your audience fits into the broad group, or social terrain. Are they the majority or the minority? Are they in a position of power or a position of weakness? Are they truly receptive to your message?

Regarding the social terrain—the aggregate of people in the arena you are operating in—identify the supporters, the opposers, the authorities/decision-makers, the neutrals, and the possible losers. Below are just some of the potential factors to consider regarding each group:

- *Supporters:* How influential are they and how can they help? Who can they influence into becoming supporters as well?

Who might they alienate? Do others know how many supporters we have and who they are?

- *Opposers:* How much influence do they have, and with whom? Can they be turned into supporters and, if so, how? If not, can they be neutralized? If they can't be neutralized, how much damage can they do? Will we gain any supporters because certain people oppose us?

- *Authorities/decision-makers:* Who holds the ultimate authority to make a decision? How can we effectively influence them and what are the politics of doing so? How is the fulfillment of our mission going to make their life easier or more difficult?

- *Neutrals:* Are they worth trying to influence? What will it take to do so? What do we lose if they become opposers?

- *Possible losers:* Unfortunately, almost no solutions satisfy everyone's needs and goals, and there may well be some who lose out no matter how hard we try to seek a win-win solution. Ask: Who will the losers be? How bad will they be affected? Can we mitigate their loss in some way? What will their reaction be if we can't mitigate the loss? Are prepared for that reaction?

- These final questions are applicable for all of the above groups, but especially for the last group:

  - Will pursuing my mission undermine or increase the trust these people have in me?

  - Will pursing my mission threaten or strengthen the ego of these people?

- Will pursing my mission threaten or enhance the sense of power these people have?

- For each question, what can I do to avoid the former and bring about the latter?

Manage your reputation and your identity.

We dramatically overestimate the accuracy with which others see us and of our ability to perceive our reputation. None of us have the time and energy to spend on truly understanding others unless we really need to, so we settle for superficial assessments and narratives without realizing it.

Yet our effectiveness lives or dies on how we are perceived by others and we can be more effective if people think positively of us. The more favorable their assessment of us, the more likely they are to help us.

The best way to find out what others think is to ask them directly or find out from someone who truly knows what others are saying. Getting actual feedback is almost always more accurate than assuming we know what others think.

Conduct an audit of your network and order people ranging from "tightly connected" (those with more access to you) to "loosely connected" to you (those with less access). Do a cross categorization of "highly influential in the organization" and "less influential." Create four general categories:

- Tightly connected/highly influential

- Tightly connected/less influential

- Loosely connected/highly influential

- Loosely connected/less influential.

Seek feedback from one or more people in each group. You can ask questions on specific topics if you like, but I find that broad and open-ended questions are the best starting point: "What do you see as my main strengths and what do you see as areas in which I could improve?"

Do not be defensive. Do not argue—you can accept the feedback or not, but you are asking people to take a risk in giving you feedback; don't make them regret it. You may feel that they identify "flaws" that are more an issue of perception than of reality. That is fine—work on changing the perception.

Thank people for their feedback; use the feedback to make positive changes. Let people know what you are trying to improve so they notice the changes when they happen. (If people don't know to look for a change, they generally won't see it.)

Be a Helper.

People want to connect with useful people who help them satisfy their needs. It is often very easy to help others at little cost to ourselves. Take every opportunity to do so. This does not mean we have to be a flatterer or subordinate our own needs to others', but doing things for others is the low-hanging fruit of ways to build influence.

- *Have you read an article you think someone else might find value in?* Share it with them. (But don't bombard people!)

- *Give positive feedback on your peers' subordinates*; let them know when you see one of their team members providing good service or exceeding expectations in some way. This benefits the subordinate (who will now see you more kindly) and it helps the boss understand the strengths of their people. (Don't offer criticisms of someone's subordinates unless asked or unless it is absolutely necessary.) Solicit feedback from others on your subordinates, and be open to the feedback.

- *Take opportunities to praise people in general.* Be genuine and don't overdo it, but life is full opportunities to point out great things that people do. This is perhaps the lowest-investment way of establishing good will with others.

- *Connect people with common interests.* Whenever you learn something about someone, think about whether you know anyone with a similar interest, has dealt with similar problems, or who could provide a solution. Offer to connect them.

- *Most of all, just be nice.* Show courtesy to others and use your manners. Put others at ease. Make people feel welcome. Do all of those things we are taught as children and expect our children to do.

Be a "go-to" person.

Similarly, develop a reputation for effectiveness and as a person who always delivers. Make it easy for people to associate you with results and they will come to you more frequently, meaning that you can go to them for favors when you need to.

Practice 'nemawashi.'

Nemawashi is the Japanese term for an informal process of reaching consensus in which one lays the foundation for an initiative by speaking individually with stakeholders to gather feedback and identify their concerns so they can be addressed in advance of a decision. This allows you to better understand the obstacles you face, who needs to be persuaded, who can be an ally and who will be an opposer, etc. It also means that people are not surprised in group meetings because they have been already made aware of problems in advance and given time to prepare for a discussion about them.

It is important when practicing *nemawashi* that you're not falling into harmful navigating patterns of spreading negative gossip or seeming duplicitous. Appropriate candor and transparency (that respects confidences) is the key to making *nemawashi* effective. You don't want to be seen as a person simply going around and telling everyone what they want to hear, or using it as an opportunity to spread gossip.

Understand that too much "authenticity" can be just as bad as too little.

The leader is playing a role—he or she is embodying the persona that followers need to see in order to feel confident in the leader's direction. Leaders who navigate skillfully know that others are projecting perceptions and expectations onto them and that it is the leader's responsibility to meet those expectations. For example, they need the leader to seem positive and confident, even in moments when the leader may not feel that way inside. They need to believe the leader is competent and has a clear vision, even when the leader isn't so sure himself. They need to believe the leader is enjoying the role she is in, even if sometimes she isn't.

Thus, leaders who skillfully navigate have a bit of the actor in them. They understand that others are seeing a mask and they must wear the mask well. The mask must not be completely false—the best actors are able to go inside themselves and find something authentic—an emotion, an experience, a posture—that fits with the character they are playing. Leaders need to use their navigating skills to understand what their followers need and then provide that persona to them while staying true to their fundamental values.

Some leaders resist this advice, falling back on the excuse of needing to be "true" to themselves. "Well, that is just who I am" is a common excuse when confronted with the need to play a role. This is a sign of an unwillingness to grow and fear of stretching oneself. I am not suggesting that the leader be duplicitous or false—I am suggesting that leaders find something in themselves that others need to see, and to show it to them for the sake of the larger goal.

Become a social power leader rather a personal power leader.

Understanding power dynamics in the group are critical for effective navigating. Leadership theorist David McClelland pointed out the difference between "personal power" leaders and "social power leaders." Fundamentally, social power leaders put the needs of the big picture and larger group ahead of themselves. This doesn't mean that your goals are not important, but they should not overshadow the group's interests. If they do, you will lose support beyond the sycophants who have tied their self-interest to yours, and even they will abandon you when it becomes convenient to do so. You can read more about this in the article titled "Power: How to Get it and Why" in this collection.

One Final Caution

The unfortunate reality that bears repeating is that even the most skillful navigators will never please everyone. The sooner you accept this, the easier it is to focus on the larger goal of the mission itself and how to accomplish it. Part of Skillful Navigation is calculating who will be disappointed, what the consequences of that disappointment are, and how to eliminate any unnecessary pain the disappointed parties feel. Understanding this last part—that people will be disappointed but there may be ways to reduce the pain caused—is critical to facing the realities that can make us better Navigators.

So, What About Rob?

Rob is still a work in progress. He received very direct feedback in a 360 assessment and has made efforts to change. However, a lot of damage has been done and he has a long way to go to restore credibility with some leadership team members, but the signs are positive. Other clients I've worked with who had similar challenges have met various fates. If they start to change early enough they can usually turn it around, but sometimes—especially in an organization with a lot of harmful navigating cultural tendencies—it can be hard to recover if the feedback is given too late.

The lesson for all of us is that it is best to start working on becoming a Skillful Navigator sooner rather than later.

You're Worth What Your Network is Worth

One of the reasons that senior executives get paid a lot of money is because they can attract high-caliber talent when they join an organization. Companies recruiting executives are not just recruiting the individual, they are recruiting the talent that individual has access to.

Companies will pay more for leaders who can recruit, develop and effectively deploy talent because such leaders get better results–a well-managed team with great players will typically outperform a well-managed team with mediocre players.

But even leaders who do a good job at developing talent in the early part of their careers can run a problem as they rise in organizations, especially those who have spent a lot of time in only one or two companies: The people they know in their company-based network may not have the ability to scale at the same rate they do. An individual leader may have the skills and attitudes to step up from running a business unit to running a business segment, but the people who work for them may not have the same abilities to make that big a leap.

This means that a leader making a big jump in scope can find themselves without a network of subordinates who can help them be successful at that new level.

Companies often have ways to try to get around this–they use recruiters, develop leadership pipelines within the company, etc.–but nothing beats the ability of a leader to reach out and access a known- and proven-entity from within their network to step in and fill a challenging role.

For these reasons, it is important for leaders to continuously develop their network both inside and outside the company for which they work.

Being able to do so involves some important attitudes and some disciplined actions.

Attitudes:

The best networkers are curious about people–they seek out what is interesting in others rather than dismissing them based on first impressions and they don't use others as audiences to talk *at*. They really want to understand others and they are willing to take the time to get to know what experiences they've had, what their interests are, what their values are, etc.

They also understand that good networks begin by doing for others rather than seeking an immediate benefit. Seek out ways to help people with no expectation of a quid pro quo. People appreciate kindnesses and gravitate toward those with a reputation for generosity. Find ways to help others and people will come to you.

Actions:

There are plenty of books and other resources available for beginning networking skills (I particularly like Heather Townsend's "Business Networking," part of the Financial Times Guides series). The suggestions below are more aimed at more-senior leaders seeking to expand their network outside their company, though almost anyone will benefit from them.

1. *Set goals for your networking and be disciplined about accomplishing them.* As with every other activity, you don't achieve much without clearly defined goals. And, you are busy and need to make the most of your efforts, so take this first step seriously. What kind of people do you want to meet, what criteria have you set to determine this? Why do you want to meet them? What can you offer in return? How many people will you meet per week, per month, etc.?

2. *Find role models and ask how they do it.* Identify other senior leaders in your organization or that you know from elsewhere who have built a strong network outside their organization. Invite them to lunch, tell them what you are trying to accomplish, and ask how they did it. Implement any useful tips they offer. Ask if there are any people they know who fit the criteria you have established and, if so, ask for an introduction.

3. *Join associations, but do so wisely.* Find an association that will consist of the kind of people you want to meet, not the people you know already. If you join, don't be passive–get involved. Join a committee, contribute to their newsletter, or speak at an event. If you attend an event, do your homework ahead of time–research people you want to meet (using social media, trade journals, or conference rosters) and be sure to get in front of them. Do not spend the event surrounded by people you already know. Set a goal for how many people you will introduce yourself to.

4. *Acknowledge others.* Read blogs and articles written by or attend talks given by the kind of people you want to meet. Contact them and let them know what you liked about what they wrote or what they talked about. Be sincere and specific. Identify an area of common interest and use that to arrange a meeting if possible–lunch or coffee when you are in the same city or at the same conference.

5. *Become a thought leader.* I cringe at the term "thought leader," but it is fitting here. You will never be able to identify all the people that would be worth meeting, and researching others takes time. Being a thought leader is a form of "pull" networking–it draws people to you from places you could have never imagined. Identify an area of expertise you have and find opportunities to write or speak about it. Thought leadership is truly a form of leadership and blogs, articles, interviews, and speeches lend authority and credibility to you. Develop a plan to publish (or speak) regularly. "Regularly" does not necessarily

mean "frequently." Opt for quality over quantity, but be sure to commit to a regular schedule and adhere to the schedule.

Cliches abound about digging your well before you are thirsty and planting seeds before you are hungry; this applies to the kind of networking that we are talking about here. If you wait until you need it, you will be too late. Nothing is worse than finding yourself in a new role, realizing you don't have the right people to support you, and not knowing where to find them.

Charisma, and How to Get More of It

Do leaders need to be charismatic in order to be successful? I don't think so, but charisma certainly helps and I think it is possible for everyone to increase their "charisma quotient." Thus, those who want to lead would do well to pay a bit of attention to this quality.

The original Greek roots of the word *charisma* refer to a gift of grace given by the divine, and this may have led to the commonly held view that, when it comes to charisma, you either have it or you don't. Anecdotally, we all know people who seem to have that X-factor that draws attention and makes people want to follow; when they enter a room, it feels like *two* people have entered. We also know people who seem to completely lack that X-factor; when they enter a room it feels as if two people *left*. These experiences with other people can reinforce the "have it or not" view of charisma.

This view is unfortunate because it often stops people from trying to become more charismatic, which then hampers the fulfillment of one's leadership potential. The rest of this post explores how we can overcome this bias and work on increasing your charisma quotient.

As with leadership, there is probably no necessary and complete model of qualities, traits, or attributes related to charisma, but I have found a list that I think serves as a good starting point. According to *New Scientist* magazine,* psychologist Ronald Riggio "has identified six traits or skills that he believes are essential: emotional expressiveness, enthusiasm, eloquence, self-confidence, vision, and responsiveness to others." Charismatic people, according to Riggio, have a good balance of all of these qualities, and having *too* much of any of them probably reduces one's personal charisma. (Robin Williams, for example, may be entertaining on stage, but how much time would you really want to spend with someone *that* expressive?)

I find that it is best to take these qualities and work on them one at a time, starting with areas in which you are already pretty good and then working your way toward the ones in which you need the most improvement. Here are some exercises to get you started:

1. *Emotional expressiveness.* Now I admit that this will feel a little silly, so do it alone. Further, it helps if you take a little time to clearly identify the benefit of increasing emotional expressiveness; it is almost impossible to make any changes that we don't believe have a true benefit. Once convinced of the benefit of increasing emotional expressiveness, start paying attention to people who demonstrate the right amount of this quality–those who show their emotions on their faces and in their gestures in a positive way. Then, take a few minutes to watch yourself in the mirror and mimic some of their facial expressions. In other words, *practice* expressing your emotions. Yes, it feels weird. Get over it. Later, when you find yourself about to interact with someone, whether it is a meeting with an individual or a group, think about what emotional state you would like to convey–is it optimism, excitement, resolve, intensity? That emotional state, and *act as if* you were someone who conveyed that emotional well. It should be subtle, don't overdue it, but let yourself go a little more than you usually would. You'll notice the change, and others will as well.

2. *Enthusiasm.* Decide *what* you are excited about. Describe, to yourself at least, *why* you are excited about it. Ask why *others* should be excited about it. Take it upon yourself to get them excited about it too. The actions and expressions will come to you naturally if you are very clear in why you are excited and why others should share that enthusiasm. Clarity of purpose and the conviction that others should share that purpose are critical to demonstrating enthusiasm.

3. *Eloquence*. The best ideas in the world are of no value unless they are well-communicated to others. Improve your vocabulary. Take an interest in words; when you encounter a word you are not absolutely sure of, take my mother's advice and "Look it up! That's why we have a dictionary." (I like Merriam-Webster's online dictionary at www.m-w.com.) Become a better writer and a better speaker. I highly recommend William Zinsser's "On Writing Well," and Roger Ailes's "You Are the Message." Buy these books today. Put them on your Kindle or iPad or Android. Read them. Start putting their lessons into use. Then read them again.

4. *Self-confidence*. True self-confidence only comes from a sense of accomplishment. Unfortunately, most people are far more accomplished than they realize, so they are less confident than they should be. I often encourage clients to conduct an "accomplishments audit." Write down a list of the things you have done and accomplished in your career. Be extensive and objective; avoid false humility, don't bother listing the blunders (this is not a recommendation to ignore areas for improvement, but that is a different exercise…). Keep the list handy. Review it frequently. Your self-confidence will rise.

5. *Vision*. It's old advice, but people still avoid it: Take some time and define your vision for your team, your organization, yourself. Visions can–and should–evolve, but we meander when we don't have an explicit vision of where we are going and why (and *meandering* is not a sign of charisma). Visions need not be grand, but they need to be *clear*. Share your vision with others at every opportunity. If anyone on your team cannot describe your vision for the team or the organization, you need to work on this more.

6. *Responsiveness to others*. The satirist Fran Lebowitz once said, "Most people don't listen, they simply wait their turn to talk." Responsiveness to others starts with actually listening to other people rather than thinking about what you would like to say, and letting them know you are listening to them through the use of *occasional* brief

paraphrases, such as "What I heard you say is…." (I used the word *occasional* on purpose; don't paraphrase everything everyone says, you will give them the creeps.) Think about what other people's needs are, and help them meet those needs.

*Young, Emma, "The X Factor," *New Scientist*, 23 June 2012.

Made in the USA
Lexington, KY
23 October 2017